MW01119530

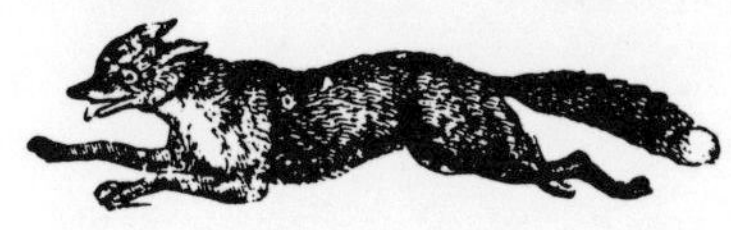

The Red Well-Read Reader

Published by

Word Play Ink
P.O. Box 186
Saranac Lake, New York 12983-4390

To Order: Call 1 (800) 685-READ

Library of Congress Cataloging in Publication Data.
McGann, Thomas Daniel
The Red Well-Read Reader
A Reader, Speller, and Vocabulary Builder
Includes stories, nursery rhymes, poems, spelling rules, and phonics charts.
1. Publishing--Textbooks, workbooks, etc.
2. Publishers--Textbooks, workbooks, etc.
I. Title
92-62808
ISBN 0-938761-13-7 HARDCOVER

DEDICATION

This book is dedicated to all who want to earn a buck and bank that buck to bring about a big return with which to do much good in turn (a la Story 141).

ACKNOWLEDGEMENTS

Words can scarcely express the debt of gratitude I owe Jack, Alice, and Brian McGann; it would take at least a lifetime to settle my account with them, an account that lacks any entries. I should also like to thank all the people who encouraged me to write this book, especially Cheryl and her three daughters Nicole, Jessica and, my precious little "girlfriend" and aptest student, Danielle. I'd like to give special thanks to my good friend J.A. Porter who believed in my talent--talent I had not even suspected I had, i.e. to make people say ha, ha . . . if only to themselves. I should also like to acknowledge some very close friends who all but wrenched my pen out of my hand so I wouldn't waste valuable ink. Them I thank for keeping the book from being published prematurely. I should also like to thank some other family members and friends for proofreading the book and for their advice and encouragement; namely, Mary Jane McGann, Pete Woods, John Rhodes, Lorin and Joan Maser, Richard Janigian, Sister Virginia Gaine, Gwen McNamee, Warren Keller, Art Atkinson, James Antos, Catherine Schlaugies, Andrea L. Young-Job, and Carol Spadaro. For business and technical support I'd like to thank Barbara and Dennis Flynn, Robert Wilkinson, James Montague, Philip Boland, John and Pattie Flynn, and Dicky "Shindog" Smith. I'd like to thank the many illustrators who are in large part responsible for making this book as good as it is; they are Stephen Provenzano, Judy Wilkinson, Mark Ruggieri, Steven Cosimano, and my special buddy--Minh Nguyen (13 years old). I'd also like to thank Rich Torrey, a syndicated cartoonist, who taught me to draw well enough to ink a few illustrations myself. I'd like to thank The Burlington Free Press and Simon & Schuster respectively for allowing W O R D P L A Y I INK. to reprint the Bucking Bronco and the Reading Kangaroo. Also I should like to acknowledge my debt to many other artists and cartoonists of the past and the present. And I should like to thank a few of my teachers who stuffed my cranium with ideas: in business Michael Falcone at New York Institute of Technology, and in publishing Lisa Healy and in graphic design Ava Barber--both at New York University. Also I should like to thank Jim Delapine for putting his finishing touch on the book's Cover. I should like to thank Pete Woods again for providing his rare talent to imitate nearly every animal sound heard on the farm or in the jungles of Africa. I should like to acknowledge the delightful and apt musical contributions of both Will Harmonic and Jim Becher. Next to last I should like to thank Jim Minnie, who recorded the readings, and over and over again edited them without tire--finding scores of extraneous sounds, improper cadences, tempos, tones, and mispronunciations--and who recorded the music and added the sound effects, creating a flawlessly done artistic product. And last I should like to thank John W. Yurchak and Stuart Manix of Wickersham Press without whose help this book wouldn't look half so good as it does.

CONTENTS

KEY NOTE

Learning to read is the first step, yearning to read the next. The first step develops a mere skill, while the other goes light years beyond cultivating the mind, building character, and revealing ages of the past and a glimpse of the future.

PREFACE

This book has been designed to help various students attain several complementary goals, the primary one reading. The principal user is any student, no matter how old or young, who would like to learn to read; that is, to read *very* well. With the assistance of a dedicated parent or teacher, students will learn to comprehend more than simple sentences, to understand various styles of expression such as irony and satire, and to glean meaning from those hidden words that lie between the lines.

A reader skimming a book can often tell whether the book has merit or not by noting just a word or two. Such practice epitomizes the reader who has learned to read well; that is, in the main, to comprehend how the world turns. Teaching developing minds to make proper inferences on the slightest sufficient information is the principal tenet of this book. Reading a bus schedule and filling out an unemployment form is nice but scarcely makes a person literate.

The Red Well-Read Reader does not offer any pabulum. It makes students reach. It shows a cross section of human activity. Thus the stories it contains touch on a wide range of topics: from baseball to economics, from virtue to crime, from current politics to ancient history, and from sheer entertainment to war.

The book has been scrutinized so as not to encourage any undesirable behavior or conduct. Nonetheless, now and then a story may use a slang word, like *nerd*. This should not, however, shock any reader. Many things used wrongly can be harmful--a knife, a gun, a car, *even* a classroom. No matter how ardently we wish our children's language to remain pure, sooner or later it will become tainted with slang, along with vulgarity and profanity. Unfortunately, the only preventive is to have children wear earplugs when not in their classrooms, and for us parents to eject all TVs from our households; this, of course, is ludicrous: for one, the dumps couldn't handle all the debris! Clearly, discretion must be taught!

Furthermore, this book vigilantly avoids prejudices. Nevertheless, it does not delude young readers to think the only differences between boys and girls are hair length, and the cut of their clothes. Nor does it pretend that all students have identical IQs, similar good looks, equal aptitudes for designing space modules, for example. And it does not hide such facts as the following: in our society people drink and sometimes get drunk, often quarrel and fight, and frequently even kill one another, and that mankind--the world over--stays in a perpetual state of war. This book, in the hands of a *competent* teacher prods students to ponder why such hostility and violence recur with almost tide-like regularity. Such thought cannot start too young!

Some educators may wonder why it is necessary to mention the deity in this or any other reading textbook. Well, the reasons are numerous, too numerous for all of them to be stated here! Some of the cardinal ones, however, are the following. One, not to mention God, when nearly everything else under the sun is mentioned, is tantamount to professing belief that there is no God. Two, belief in God has historically been, as it is today, or should be, mankind's greatest determinant of behavior (e.g. love thy neighbor as thyself). Three, children are in dire need of spiritual sustenance. One does not need to be a child psychologist to see the void in their hearts, a mere look at their faces suffices. Today, beginning at the tenderest ages, our children have already grown jaded, full of skepticism, pessimism, and cynicism.

Notwithstanding--this book contains no prayers. It is not a prayer book, it is not a religious book: it only mentions *God*, mentions *prayer*, mentions *Christ*--mentions *Christ* as an historical figure that has influenced humankind (believers and non believers as well) incomparably more so than any other figure who has graced this planet.

Despite the want of teaching right from wrong, this book does not pretend to teach morality. It cannot, no textbook can. This job is exclusively the teacher's. Consequently the ultimate benefit of this book is commensurate with the teacher's capability.

The Red Well-Read Reader may be likened to a symphony: well orchestrated, practiced, and conducted--the result is uplifting and edifying; otherwise, it is not.

The book's goal, to be sure, is to teach students to THINK--not *what* to think but *how* to think--thus, ipso facto, every decoder becomes a discriminating reader. What is more, the student ultimately realizes that clear thinking involves not just the mind but also the heart.

Introduction

What Does It Do?
For Whom Is It Designed?

Not *dumbed down*, *The Red Well-Red Reader* combines phonics and *Look and Say* providing a step-by-step, hard and fast superior method to teach reading thoroughly. What's more, its stories make the subject thought provoking and fun--fun to learn, fun to teach. It's fun mainly because it's thought provoking. Many of its stories can be read again and again with profit.

Although foremost a *reader*, it is also a *speller* and a *vocabulary builder*. *The Red Well-Read Reader* is so efficacious that it can teach these three subjects exclusive of other books. This text, however, should not be viewed as an end in itself but as a catalyst that propels students into a higher orbit of learning.

When through with this book, children should have sufficient knowledge to read almost anything and be well on their way in becoming proficient spellers. Because this book contains nearly every single-syllable word of the language, and because a large portion of these words is used in the context of the stories--students will be expanding their vocabularies dynamically. Vocabulary being a measure of one's intelligence, this feature is quite important! As a reader and as a vocabulary builder, this book defies the trend of a controlled, limited vocabulary leapfrogging over basal readers. Its stories are challenging to the brightest students, while neither threatening nor overwhelming to the slower students. Every story is designed to make readers *think*, unlike most basal readers which often contain no more than drivel.

Any child, say, from six to adulthood may be taught by *The Red Well-Read Reader*. Even younger children may be weaned on this book. The only prerequisite is that the student have some familiarity with such everyday words as *mom, dad, who, which, is, are, good, bad, you, I, should, love* and so on. Nursery rhymes, flash cards and simple stories are the tools to teach these words. This book is designed for all the following readers:

- **First and Second Graders**
- **Younger Children (limited usage)**
- **High Schoolers in Remedial Programs**
- **Foreign Students learning English as a Second Language (or merely working on pronunciation)**
- **Adults in Literacy Programs**
- **Special Education Students with dysfunctions like Dyslexia &**
- **The Reading Public**

Because this book covers virtually every utterable sound of the English language, it ipso facto covers every monosyllabic word as well as the various spellings thereof. Therefore it should be of some value even to teachers who already are well-read.

The greater number of stories are written either in rhythmic prose or verse; thus they are naturally funny. Students will laugh even at stories they don't fully understand. There are many such stories. But this feature does not detract; contrarily, it enhances learning. It is the *sine qua non.* This just mentioned expression is apropos: one need not know Latin to venture a guess at its meaning. The loss of understanding is inconsequential even if the guess be way off; besides, the next time the phrase is seen it will be better understood.

When a youngster begins to read he or she is thrilled just to pronounce the printed words on a page. This is a giant step, perhaps the biggest step most of us will ever take. It is called "decoding." Comprehending, on the other hand, differs markedly from decoding. Comprehension is like an appreciation of wine, developing slowly, becoming more refined over time; whereas decoding, a much less complicated skill, can be learned by everyone inside and out, upside down, thoroughly, completely, totally at a very early age, say five or six.

In essence this method focuses on decoding and lets comprehension alone, to come later, as it may, in its own time. By and large, just one new sound, or phonological structure, is presented per story. Nonetheless, some of the stories are rather sophisticated. Depending on maturity and aptitude, each student will grasp some, most, or all, the content at his or her individual pace. Learning the rudimentary mechanics, on the other hand, is done thoroughly, step by step, together as a class. Students, therefore, shall not be flustered by however fast the text is being covered. Even the slowest learners will be able to keep pace as they learn the mechanics, while the faster students will be engrossed in the story. Each student benefits according to his or her aptitude. With this method there is no point where a slow student might get discouraged, give up hope, and quit trying altogether. Nor is there any point where a bright student might become bored, because the task remains challenging throughout the entire 361 stories.

How Should The Book Be Used?

A couple of points must be discussed before going into the 5-Step Method. The first point, pertaining primarily to preschool-age students, is obvious though sometimes overlooked: printing or penmanship should be taught concurrently with reading--one reinforcing the other. The second point: as students begin decoding they should be guided to other books, preferably to literature.

The 5-Step Method

<u>Step One</u> **Go over the Phonics Charts 1, 2, 3 and 4 in the back of the book.** This should be repeated over and over until students gain a working knowledge of beginning consonantal building blocks and--especially important for foreign students--the variable sounds of the hybrid *y* vowel.

<u>Step Two</u> **Study the second section of the book, 361 charts of "Families."** This step is to be made in a more or less random fashion, picking, let's say, those Families corresponding respectively to Stories 1, 4 and 20--all of which have a *short a* sound. Then the teacher might move to a few Families with a *long a* sound, then next through the other eighteen classifications.

These words may be recited by the class in unison, or by the students individually, one student reading the first word then another student reading the second word and so on, or in any other manner you, the teacher, may choose. This exercise allows students to see how words are formed: most words, as you know, are formed by combining a consonant or a consonant blend with an ending composite of one or two vowels and another consonant or consonant blend. The teacher decides how long this step should extend before taking the next step. Discretion is necessary here to allow for variance from class to class.

<u>Step Three</u> **Read, or recite, the particular family chart that corresponds to a story you've predetermined to read. Make sure that the meanings of the various words, especially those used in the context of the story, are somewhat understood. Then read that story. Then reread that story several more times. Next you should ask questions about it--such as, "Could it be true?" "Why?"** BY KNOWING THE MEANING OF THE BOLD WORDS, STUDENTS ARE ABLE TO MAKE GUESSES AT THOSE OTHER WORDS IN REGULAR PRINT, SOME OF WHICH ARE DIFFICULT--THUS ARE SYLLABICATED. <u>This, certainly, is one of the most significant features of the book!</u>

<u>Step Four</u> **Read the remaining 360 stories in the same manner as Step Three.** It does not matter where you start or whether you follow any particular order, because no story is much harder than any other story to decode. The only thing that does matter here is that all 361 stories be covered. Collectively, the stories, along with their related charts, contain all the building blocks of the English language--virtually every monosyllabic word.

Because the stories stay at the same level of difficulty from start to finish--any student who after being sick, say for a week, a month or even longer, upon returning to class can fall back into step as though he or she had not missed a single class. What was missed during the student's absence can easily be made up later without rush or anxiety. The absent student has not missed any concepts, the only things missed are bits of phonetic knowledge and reading practice.

Step Five **Study the "Derivatives," the third and last principal part of the book, comprising 361 charts of derivations.** (This step should not be taken until months after the stories have been started.) Here the focus should be on spelling and some of the many peculiarities of the language.

Why Is Studying "Families" and "Derivatives" Invaluable?

Turning to Family 1, for example, you will see that one word, *Arab*, is an anomaly pronounced unlike the other words in this family. The corresponding derivative chart (D1) shows one word, *cabby*, with an alternative spelling, *cabbie*. There are also some rather difficult words here--for example, *fabulous* and *laboratory*. And there is another peculiarity here with *rabbit* and *habit*: no spelling rule explains why the former word has two *b's* and the later just one *b*. Such words are best learned by mnemonic aids. In the family and derivative charts corresponding to Story 2 we see much more. The family chart shows the phonetic /ak/ spelled in three ways--*ack*, *ak*, and *aque*; the derivative chart has it spelled in yet two more ways--*ac* and *aq*, as shown in the medial position of several words. Incidentally, *bivouac* is included here not just for its *ac* sound but also for its phonetic /w/, spelled *ou*. *Khaki*, is also placed here to show the unique position of its silent *h*.

Almost all consonantal sounds are found at the beginning of words. As noted earlier, these sounds are listed in Charts 2 and 3 in the back of the book. Some few sounds, however, like *rm* and *ck*, do not start a word, thus are seen only randomly here and there throughout the book.

As you turn the family-chart pages you will see homonyms--e.g., *you* and *ewe*; you will see heteronyms also, which actually are two words spelled the same though having different sounds and different meanings--*wind, read,* and *tear* are some examples; and you will see some other words like *rage*, *chief*, and *land* which have one pronunciation when standing alone and a different one altogether when part of a bigger word as in *ga•rage, mis•chief*, and *Hol•land.*

By seeing derivational forms repeated time and time again students will learn various spelling rules, such as those to govern when to add *s* or *es* to make a noun plural, when to drop the final *e* of an adjective and add *ly* in its place to get its adverbial form, and when to double the final consonant of a verb to make its past tense. In the back of the book there is a complete list of basic spelling rules.

Lastly, students will learn about the most confusing sound of the language--one, I believe, that is more confusing than the other sounds altogether. This culprit is sometimes called the universal or colorless vowel, but is best known as the schwa. Because phonics can neither be taught nor talked about neatly, for eons the schwa has been purposely misclassified as a *short u*. In monosyllabic words the schwa is indeed preponderantly spelled with a *u*; in multi-syllabic words; however, it is spelled with any one of the five common vowels, which includes the *u*: it is the *a* in *ago*, the *e* in *system*, the *i* in *vanity*, the *o* in *comply*, and, of course, the *u* in *rebut*. It is also found in digraphs like *oi* in *porpoise*, to mention just one of many. Unquestionably this practice has kept phonics simple--but too simple, I believe, to have been much help considering all the confusion it has created. It leaves many students bewildered, questioning their ability and despairing because of "half-truth" rules which fail to cover the language thoroughly. Studying the orthography of the English language without the schwa is no more possible than learning physics without mathematics or medicine without chemistry.

This omission is undoubtedly the primary reason that phonics has never gained universal acceptance. All of us who read have learned to do so by phonics. This is fact whether or not we are cognizant of it. Either we were taught phonics (by a teacher), or we learned it on our own unawares. Unfamiliarity with this critical characteristic is probably the biggest stumbling block to reading, let alone spelling. It must be emphasized, then re-emphasized over and over, again and again.

How Fast Can A Class Cover This Book?
What Should Be The Expectations For The Users Of It?

Depending on the class and the time allocated to it, *The Red Well-Read Reader* should take one or two school years.

Even if the students should understand only half of what they read, they will be rocketed light years beyond their contemporaries who are sputtering along with basal readers, few of which have even a semblance of a "scientific approach," and spellers that are without any approach except a random one.

The author hopes that this text will help develop an appetite for books, and enkindle an appreciation of the English language that grows keener and keener as students strive to better understand the world about them and to communicate clearly that which they each individually observe and experience.

INDEX

Ē

ĒR̃

R̃

Ĭ

167. int . . . Her Hospital Stint
168. ip . . . . On an Ocean Trip
169. ipt . . . . No Script!
170. iss . . . . The Swiss Miss
171. ish . . . A Tasty Dish
172. isk . . . Frisked
173. ism . . . Holy Chrism
174. isp . . . Don't Lisp These "Isps"
175. ist . . . . A Lovers' Tryst
176. it . . . . Pig on a Spit
177. itch . . . The Fritches
178. ith . . . A Myth
179. ix . . . . Kicks at Six
180. izz . . . . Liz Is a Dizz

ŋ

181. ing . . . Bells Shall Ring
182. ink . . . The Missing Link
183. inct . . . The "Inct" Precinct
184. inx . . . Mr. and Mrs. Finks

Ī

185. y . . . . . Don't Cry
186. ye . . . . "Aye, Aye"
187. igh . . . Climbing High
188. ie . . . . A Pie-Eating Contest
189. ibe . . . Bribed
190. ice . . . . A Thinking Device
191. ide . . . The Young Bride
192. iet . . . . Cry It
193. ife . . . . Strife is Rife!
194. ike . . . Alike
195. ile . . . . A Lady of Inimitable Style
196. ild . . . . A Precious Child
197. ime . . . A Nursery Rhyme
198. ine . . . At Nine
199. ind . . . Develop Your Mind
200. ipe . . . Blood of Every Type
201. ire . . . . The Brave Squire
202. ite . . . . The Writer's Plight
203. ight . . . The Flight of the Playwright
204. ithe . . . Not Blithesome
205. ive . . . How Success Arrives
206. ize . . . Unwise

AH or AW

207. ah . . . . At the Spa
208. ob . . . . They Began to Sob
209. ock . . . Father Bach
210. od . . . . On Cape Cod
211. odge . . Rodge
212. og . . . . Outside of Prague
213. om . . . After the Prom
214. alm . . . Palm Sunday
215. omp . . Back to the Swamp
216. on . . . . John
217. op . . . . Pig Slop and Soda Pop
218. osh . . . Josh
219. ot . . . . Overtaking the . . . . Penobscots
220. otch . . Scotch
221. oth . . . The Goths
222. ox . . . . Albert Knox
223. age . . . Nearly Every "Azh"

AW

224. aw . . . The Crows that Can't Caw
225. aud . . . Thanks to Maude
226. off . . . . Don't Scoff
227. oft . . . In the Loft
228. awl . . . He Started a Brawl
229. all . . . . The Fall Ball
230. auld . . In Times of Auld
231. alk . . . A Balk
232. alt . . . Whose Fault?
233. altz . . . The Schmaltzy Waltz
234. olve . . The Crime Was Solved
235. awn . . Sean
236. aunch . The Boat Launch
237. aunt . . His Last Jaunt
238. ond . . . The Blond
239. ong . . . Right Is Wrong
240. onk . . . Verbal Honky-Tonk
241. oss . . . Haus
242. ost . . . Embossed
243. aught . Fraught with Trickiness
244. ause . . Santa Claus

STORIES

STORIES

Ă

Story 1

Nabbed

I don't like to be stared at!

"No thanks, no sweets!" said **Dr. McNabb**. "Not a **slab**, not even a **dab**. You see I am trying to lose some **flab**. Therefore I eat just **crab** and I drink just **Tab**. Now please bring me my bill, or call it a **tab** if you will. But let's not **confab**, or in other words--**gab**, for I *must* hasten back to my **lab**."

As his waitress left to tally his **tab**, **McNabb** continued to **blab**, saying something about taking a **stab** . . . at not paying his **tab**.

Then he fled outside and quickly **grabbed** a **cab**. But thanks to the police he was soon **nabbed**. A criminal **tabbed**. From then on his life was dreary and **drab**.

<u>*Story 2*</u>

The Wacky Hack

Jack drives a **hack** checkered white and **black**. While he drives he loves to **yak** and smoke cigarettes by the **pack**. He calls all the guys "**Jack**," and all the gals "**Mac**"--even though not long ago one gal gave him such a **whack** that he landed **smack** on his **back** and broke his **sa-cro-il-i-ac**.

Despite his wife's **flak**, **Jack** often goes to the **track** where he searches in vain for the winning **knack**, then later drowns his sorrow with a sudsy six-**pack**.

Being broke, he lives in a **wracked shack**. Having no bed, he sleeps in a **haystack**. And having no hangers, he **tacks** his **slacks** in plaster **cracks**.

Good gracious! How **Jack's** life **lacks**!

Story 3

Tact

If you'd have **tact**, then thoughtful is how you'd **act**. With anger, you'd not **re-act**, smiles not tears you'd **ex-tract**, and rash words you'd need not **re-tract**.

As a matter of **fact**, the way you would **act** would surely make a most favorable **im-pact**.

Story 4

Brad

Brad wasn't such a nice **lad**. He seldom made his mom or **dad glad**. And as he grew older he turned awfully **bad**. Girls called him a good-for-nothing **cad**. And his teacher said he couldn't even **add**.

Of course, **Brad** never did become a **grad**, yet a job he still should have **had**. But lazy **Brad** refused so much as look at a **want ad**. Now the foolish boy is terribly, terribly **sad**.

HELP WANTED

Trainee -- Must know ABC's and XYZ's. Must be able to count to 100. Must know up from down and left from right. Knowing right from wrong would be helpful too. Call 1 (800) LUV-WORK.

☞ See *Stories 38 & 39*

Story 5

Madge

"But, Officer," said **Madge**. "I must live the life of a **cadge**." "But **Madge**," said the officer. "It's unlawful to bum so much as a **fadge**[1]. Therefore, dear girl, I arrest you by the authority of my **badge**."

"Oh, Officer, why do you **badger** this helpless **cadger**?"

1) A potato pie.

Story 6

A Hearty Horse Laugh

The zebra gave the zoo **staff** some bitter **gaff**. "Why do the **giraffe** and the baby buffalo **calf** get oats when all I get is the **chaff**? This is an out-rageous **gaffe**!"

The em-bar-rassed **staff** replied looking at their **graph**, "Apologies to you, it was indeed a snafu[1]! From now on you'll get oats, and a portion of an extra **half**."

"But that's not enough, **staff**!" said the zebra, letting out a hearty horse **laugh**. "I want white or red vino, and every day a **half carafe**!"

1) Situation Normal All Fouled Up.

Story 7

Daft

Bill said: "Would you like to sail in my **craft**?"

Sue said: "No, I don't like any art or **craft**!"

Bill said: "Would you rather white water in my river **raft**?
You may sit in either the fore or the **aft**."

Sue said: "No! I have a **raft** of other things to do this sunny
Saturday **aft--after-noon**!"

Bill said: "But, Sue, soon I'll be taken in the Army **draft**!"

Sue said: "**Draft**, **draft**! My father drinks nothing but Miller **draft**, and I'm forever writing or sketching a **draft**. Besides, don't you know, one could catch a cold in a **draft**?"

Bill angrily said: "Geez! She's **daft**!"

Sue comically said: "Cheese? She's **Kraft**?"

Then Sue, and then Bill . . . **laughed** and **laughed**.

Story 8

The "Nag" and the "Scalawag"

There once lived a young **wag** who used to **brag** how happy he was **stag**.

However there came a **snag**, he got "hooked" by **Mag**. Shortly thereafter, he says, all she did was **nag** and call him a good-for-nothing **scalawag**.

He pro-tes-ted, "I don't like this un-be-fit-ting **tag**. But for sure--you're an old **hag**, and you've made my life a miserable **drag**."

"You silly **wag**!" she replied. "You make me **gag**. Right from the start you made our mar-riage **flag**!"

Story 9

The Exam

Tomorrow **Pam** and **Sam** will take an **exam** far off in **Amsterdam**. They will board a noisy **wham**, **bam**, **slam tram** on whose tracks they'll cross a **dam**.

They'll eat candied **yams**, crackers **graham**, and sandwiches of **jam**, **ham**, **Spam**, and **lamb**--as they **cram** for their final spelling **exam**.

☞ See *Story 45 & 46*

Story 10

The Little Tramp

Judy and Sue chose to **camp** near a boat **ramp**. As night was setting in they were reading by their ker-o-sene **lamp** when they heard something or someone **stamp**! Next they heard a pair of jaws **champ**!

At that they knew it was just the park **scamp**, and shooed away that bear **tramp**.

Story 11

The Legend of Dan McGann

Dan McGann is one heck of a **man**! While driving his **van** he **can** eat a bowl of **bran**, drink coke--**can** after **can**--faster **than** anyone **can**, cook steak in a **pan**, book **scan**, teach the **Can-Can** to **Anne** and **Fran**--and even discuss a **clan-des-tine plan** with his Cool (Ice Cool) Dude and Dudette **clan**.

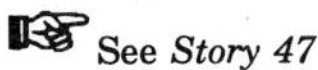
See *Story 47*

Story 12

To France

For weeks **Vance** was in a **trance**. He dreamt of going to **France**. He wanted so much to get a **glance** at knights who wield a **lance** while riding horses that **prance**. Moreover, he wanted to see the Pa-ri-sian show girls **dance**.

But would his boss take a blocking **stance**?

No! To his surprise he was given a pay **advance**. So he rushed to tell his wife **Nance**, who thrilled at the **chance** of **romance**. Then they were off to **France** as though biting **ants** were in their **pants**.

Story 13

On The Ranch

The thought of work made Billy-Joe **blanch**. However, rather than starve, he took a job on a Dude **ranch**.

He had to pick almonds from the **branch**, which he placed in a pot to **blanch**. He also picked fruits to **blanch**.

After a few months, when the hot sun made his clothes **blanch** and his hair **blanch**, he quit and married--you guessed it . . . **Blanche**.

Story 14

A Grand Band

The vi-o-lin-ist fixed his music on his **stand**; the pi-an-ist sat ready at her **Baby Grand**; the maestro raised his wand in his **hand**--then, on cue, the **band** played in such a way that tears flowed from every lach-ry-mal **gland**.

But the ap-plause was anything but **bland**. **And** all agreed that this **band** sounded **grand** and played as well as any other **band** in the entire **land**.

Story 15

Fang Sics The Gang

Rita couldn't sleep. The screen door went **whang** . . . **bang**; pots 'n' **pans** cling **clang**; and silverware, ting **tang**. Now and again the phone **rang**. Outside, a flock of geese honked, "**yang yang**." And last and loudest a trash **gang** yelled crass **slang**.

At her wit's end, Rita cried, "Sic 'em, **Fang**!" And in a flash, her dog **sprang spang** into that ter-ri-fied trash **gang**!

☞ See *Story 50*

1st OFFENSE

2nd OFFENSE

Story 16

Thrown in the County Tank

In horror people **shrank** as two men robbed the National **Bank**. One took the money while the other guarded the **flank**.

A witness (whom we **thank** for being so **frank**) said, "One was **lank** and the other a **tank**. And phew! they were **rank**! I mean to say--they **stank**!"

E-ven-tu-al-ly hound dogs found the two, named **Frank** and **Hank**, hiding along a river **bank** in a cave dingy and **dank**.

In court, **Frank** said, "It was merely a silly **prank**. My gun fired nothing but a **blank**. Besides, the money is insured by the **bank**."

The jury didn't think this was a **prank**, silly or otherwise, and tossed the two in the county **tank**.

Story 17

"Who Can't?"

"Who **can't**?" said the **ant**. "I **grant** you that I **shan't** say **can't**. I'll climb any **plant**. I don't care if the fo-li-age is **scant**. I don't care if its stem has a sharp **slant**.

"And I don't care how hard I might **pant**, nor how loudly Farmer Brown might **rant** his ad-mon-ish-ing **chant**."

Story 18

Viciously Slapped

In World War II many American **chaps** were caught in boobie **traps**. Around their wrists and ankles irons were **clapped**. Their faces were **slapped**, their backs **strapped**, and their wounds left **unwrapped**.

For failure to **rap** or to reveal any plan or **map**, they were fed just baby **pap** and maybe a leftover **scrap**.

Some **snapped**. For trying to escape many were **zapped**. Others died because their energy was **sapped**--often taking a shivering **nap** without even a blanket in which to **wrap**.

☞ See *Story 52*

Story 19

A Behavioral Lapse

Under the church **apse** Sister Helga turned and said, "Young **chaps**! You ought to have *off* your **caps**! Now *place* them in your **laps**.

"I warn you, another be-hav-ior-al **lapse** will get your face several **slaps** and, **perhaps**, your knuckles as many **raps**."

And as it happened--Tyrone and Tyrell got their **raps** for talking about **Pabst** and the art of shooting **craps**.

Story 20

Apt To Be Tongue Trapped

Likely or suited means **apt**
To become suited means **adapt**
Covered is the same as **wrapped**
And **wrapped** is the same as **wrapt**
Knocked is the same as **rapped**
But **rapped** is not the same as **rapt**
Enchanted, though, is the same as **rapt**

Story 21

Ass to Sass

There is:

A hee-haw **ass**

A fish **bass**

A metal **brass**
A com-mand-ing **brass**
An im-pu-dent **brass**
A dull **class**
A col-lege **class**
And a stupid **crass**

A deadly **gas**
A natural **gas**
A pe-tro-le-um **gas**
A looking **glass**
An op-ti-cal **glass**
A crys-tal **glass**
And a drinking **glass**

A green **grass**
A musical **Blue Grass**
A Kentucky blue **grass**
A Bermuda **grass**
And a zoysia **grass**

A good-looking **lass**
A large **mass**
A bulky **mass**
A nuptial **mass**
A requiem **mass**
A permission **pass**
An advancing **pass**
A refusing **pass**

An attempting **pass**
A flirtatious **pass**
A mountain **pass**
And back talking **sass**

Story 22

"Succotash!"

Two men held up First Federal and took all its **cash** and fled in a mad **dash**. Down the wet streets they **plashed**, rain striking their windshield with a blinding **splash**. Rounding a turn, they spun out of control and **crashed**.

Somehow they managed to flee into a thick forest of pine and **ash**. They were soon caught, although not before hiding the **cash**.

Later in court the judge's teeth began to **gnash**. Then he shouted, "Unless you sur-ren-der the **cash** now, you will get **thrashed** and **lashed**."

Horrified, the two men cried out together, "**Succotash**, Judge! Surely, you may have back *all* that **cash**!"

Story 23

Next Time You'll Ask!

Not bothering to **ask**, Nicole tapped her dad's **cask** and poured wine into a goat-skin **flask**. Then off to the beach she went to **bask** in the sun and have some fun.

Upon her return home her dad said, "You didn't **ask**! You took wine from the cellar **cask**. I'd expect no better from a thief with a **mask**. For this you'll get a pu-ni-tive **task**!"

<u>*Story 24*</u>

A Chasm

When a person **has 'em**--
That is one after another muscle **spasm**--
And if his masseuse shows no **en-thu-si-asm**
To help him **pass 'em,**
Then the patient might blurt out cutting **sar-casm**,
And between the two may come an unfriendly, unbridgeable **chasm**.

<u>*Story 25*</u>

Death By An Asp

When Sarah was about to file a gate **hasp**,
She reached down to **clasp** hold of a metal **rasp**
But there in the grass was a poi-son-ous **asp**.
It bit her and made her lose her **grasp**.
Within minutes she had breathed her final **gasp**.

<u>*Story 26*</u>

Last

At the start of the race the sailboat broke **fast** on the ocean so **vast**. **Passing** a reef, she gave her horn a **blast**; however, a fisherman's **cast** caught hold of the her **mast** and held **fast**.

All the other boats hurried **past**--thus this sailboat came in **last**.

Story 27

A Brat

"**Pat**, don't be a **brat**! Take off our **hat**, wipe your feet on the **mat**, and **scat**. The next time you mistreat our kitty **cat**, we won't **chat**. I'll treat you like a **rat**, spank you with a bed **slat**, or even cook you in a **vat**. Tit for **tat**! Got **that**?"

☞ See *Story 54*

Story 28

The Catch

Through a **hatch** that didn't **latch**, sneaked the Cookie Monster into the house. Being dark, he lit a **match**. His **snatch**--cookies, a whole **batch**.

He left through the same **hatch**, then ran di-rect-ly into a briar **patch**. He received a nasty tell-tale **scratch** and lost a sneaker that the police were able to **match**--with which they later made *their* **catch**.

Story 29

Mother's Wrath

Jane's mother spanked her with a wooden **lath**, then said, "From now on you'll walk a narrow **path**. You had better never again flunk **math**!

"For in-ci-ting my **wrath**, starting tonight you'll go to bed right after your **bath**."

☞ See *Story 56*

Story 30

What *Do* We Have!

Do you know that--

A cut, a scrape, or a scratch should **have** a dressing of **salve**?

Do you know that--

A cow can **have** or **calve** a calf? And if she **have** two, she has calfs or **calves**?

Do you know that--

The lower fleshy part of the leg is also called a calf, and similarly the two are called calfs or **calves**?

Do you know that--

An apple may be **halved**, then two **halves**, not halfs, is what you **have**?

And do you know that--

Zero is a number that you may **halve**, but if you **halve** zero--zero is still what you **have**?

Story 31

Tax Time

Relax, Max
You've made a profit on your **flax**
And now you must pay your **tax**
And don't be **lax**
And don't slash them with an **ax**
Nor say to me, "Hey, dude, mind ya own **beeswax**!"

Story 32

The Razzmatazz

Some say that it's **La Paz**
But it's New Orleans that **has**
A band known **as**
The **Razzmatazz**
Named for playing
Razzle, dazzle jazz
And that be some kind of **Jazz**, man

Ā

Story 33

On The Quay

Down by the **bay** at the break of **day**
Go **Jay** 'n' **Kay**, so happy and **gay**.
To watch the golden **ray** color the dawn's **gray**,
Exposing ships coming home and going **away**.
Soon sailboats are on **display**
Merrily **they** bob and **they sway**,
Next swallows leave their cliffs of **clay**,
Singing on their airy **way**, so as if to **say**:
That life is but an endless **day**
How cheerfully we ought to **play**
How thankfully we ought to **pray**

Story 34

Fay Says She's Fey

Fay claims to be **fey** and **soothsay**. But on the in-no-cent she'll **prey**.

She'll have you pick a card, **say** a **trey**, then try to guess your **birth-day**. She **may say** that your lucky month is **May**, that you might win a **Chev-ro-let**, or that you'll marry a **Jay** or a **Ray**. She **may** even **say** that you'd better start to **pray** for you'll soon return to **clay**.

All for which she'll make you dearly **pay**.

Story 35

Neighing And Braying

Why does the horse **neigh** and the donkey **bray**? Is it because of the road's rugged **way**? Or is it because of the weight of their **sleigh**--a ton it must **weigh**?

Heigh! Could it be **they** eat just grass when what **they** really want is **hay**?

Story 36

Ace

The horse's name is **Ace**, for on his **face** there is a **race** with an "A"-shaped **trace**. And even though he has to wear a knee **brace** with a two-foot **lace**, **Ace** always sets a fast **pace**, and with **grace** usually wins first **place**.

Story 37

The Dog Chase

Because the mailman had to squirt Bow Wow with **mace**, and because Bow Wow knocked over a flower **vase**, chewed up third **base** and a **briefcase**--her master put her in the safe **place** of a dog **chase**.

Story 38

Love In Second Grade

I shall never, never **trade** those times, those wonderful times in second **grade**.

Do you remember that cool mountain lake in which we used to **wade**? our picnics within a willow's **shade**? and how we loved selling **lemonade**?

Do you remember that forest **glade**? It was there you gave me a precious **jade**, and I in turn promised my love would never **fade**!

☞ See *Story 4*

Story 39

The Overpaid Maid

There once was a **staid** old **maid** who no one could say was a gay **blade**. She never wore makeup, nor did she ever put her hair up in a **braid**.

To the woman of the house, she was no **aid**: beds she never **made**, and ironing she would always **evade**. For hours messes usually **stayed**, cock-roaches making their daily **raid**, as she lay sleeping in the **shade**.

Nevertheless, she was handsomely **paid**: $10 an hour is what she **made**.

☞ See *Story 4*

Story 40

The Waif

When jets made a bombing **strafe**, the child received only a minor skin **chafe**; but she lost her parents, her house, and the money in her family's **safe**.

And so she became a wandering **waif** and lived a life so **unsafe**.

Story 41

Sage Counsel

Paige, your daddy's counsel is **sage**. He told you to start studying at an early **age**.

This means **page** after **page** you must turn so as to free your mind from ig-no-rance's **cage**. Someday, then, you might become a Senate **page**, later an actress on **stage**. But in whatever you choose to **engage**, do not measure success by your salary or **wage**. Let happiness be the much better **gauge**.

Story 42

Jake's Wake

To keep busy Bob fed the duck and **drake**, George **raked** the lawn, and Sarah **baked** a **cake**.

Their hard work had helped to keep their minds off **Jake**, but good humor they could no longer **fake**. You see, **Jake** was bitten by a poi-son-ous **snake.** And now his friends have broken down in a tearful **quake** at the dead boy's **wake**.

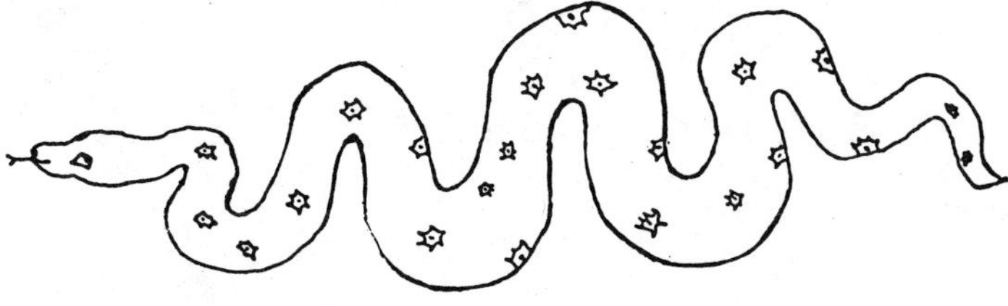

Story 43

A Whale of a Tale

Gail and **Dale** went to the **vale**, or call it a **dale**, to gather heads of **kale**. There they drank so much **ale** that their vigor soon started to **fail**, their color turning **pale**. Then--believe it or not--they said they saw a **sailfish sailing** in a **gale** that was bigger than Moby Dick or any other **whale**.

Story 44

To Jail

Out of season **Abigail** shot a **quail** and a long-necked **rail**. She also stole some U.S. **Mail**.

Officer Bale cried out, "We must **nail** this **female**. We must put a **tail** on her **trail**."

E-ven-tu-al-ly they did catch her shop-lift-ing goods in a lunch **pail**. She pleaded, "But, your Honor, a cold prison will make my health **fail**, for I am already so **frail**."

The judge replied, "**Wail** as you will, **Abigail**, but I shan't lower your **bail**, you'll remain in my **jail**."

Story 45

Football Fame

If a boy wants to play football, and if he is good at the **game**--then he might gain a well-known **name** and have trophies to **enframe**.

But a loss could be his **blame** and result in **shame**. Or worse, he could be rendered **lame**.

All the **same**, if his mind be properly **framed** and his heart **inflamed**, then he should add to the **fame** of a u-ni-ver-si-ty such as **Notre Dame**.

☞ See *Story 9*

Story 46

The Lame Game

'Tis the **blame** of the hunter's poor **aim** that he has no **game** to **claim**.

And what's more, what a **shame**!--now the poor little deer is **maimed**, and it will for-ever hobble **lame**.

☞ See *Story 9*

Story 47

The Crazy Dane

While strolling on a jungle **lane**, Tarzan and **Jane** came upon a **Dane** who was ap-par-ent-ly not **sane**. He was tugging on a lion's **mane**, poking the beast with a **cane**.

But their efforts to save him were in **vain**. The lion sprung on the **Dane**, and quickly the man's life began to **wane**.

☞ See *Story 11*

Story 48

Saving His Brain

Cain is a **swain**[1] living in rural **Spain**.

He says, "The problem with **plane** geometry is that it's much more complex than **plain**. To me this stuff is a physical **drain** and a big **pain** to my overworked **brain**.

"My efforts to learn have all been in **vain**. Besides, what can I **gain**? Yet I am **fain** to **strain**, for otherwise my teacher will split my **brain** in **twain**."

1) A country boy.

Story 49

Impoliteness Reigns

When **Skip Lane** ordered steak but was served **chow mein**, he said aloud, "I must **complain**!"

He did, only to have his waitress **exclaim**, "Buddy boy, you're lucky to be in out of the **rain**."

Lane--shocked by this ill-mannered **vein** of **disdain**--said, "I find my temper hard to **rein**. Never have I seen such im-po-lite-ness **reign**, es-pe-cial-ly here in **Du-quesne**, and in a public **do-main**.

"No tip shall I tip you," Skip said to **Jane**, "for ev-i-dent-ly you're already quite tipsy on **cham-pagne**!"

Story 50

Home On The Range

It is not so **strange**
To see buffalo **range**
Near the Rocky Mountain **range**.
You might think that some have the **mange**,
But it's just an old coat that they're trying to **ex-change**.

☞ See *Story 15*

Story 51

The Habit of the Saint

There once lived a **saint** who daily showed **self-restraint**. She could tolerate the word **ain't**, but at hearing a cuss word she would nearly **faint**.

Holy images she would often **paint**. And she prayed for those whose hearts were **faint**.

Her guard, not even the devil could **feint**; therefore, her virtue no blemish could **taint**.

Story 52

Don't Jape The Ape

Although the sign read, "DON'T **JAPE**[1] THE **APE**," the fool monkeyed the **ape**, taunt-ing him with a tasty **crepe**, strik-ing him with a **grape.**

Quite angered, the **ape** yanked his bars plump out of **shape** and caught the boy trying to **escape**.

With mouths **agape**, the frightened crowd watched as the **ape** con-vinc-ing-ly settled the **scrape**.

☞ See *Story 18* 1) Tease.

Story 53

Faced with Fattening Paste

In **haste**
The chef mixed a doughy **paste**,
Which on a roast he'd **baste**.
But all was a **waste**,
For the rich **taste**
Was too much for every dieter's not-so-slim **waist**.

Story 54

A Spate of Prate

Can-di-date Kate stood on a **crate** and began her **spate** praising her running **mate**.

"We fully back the Dem-o-crat-ic **slate**. And let me **state** that we truly love your e-lec-tor-al **state**.

"Taxes we shall **abate**, and at a fast **rate**. In fact, we shall **in-i-ti-ate** a tax **rebate**. However, we promise never to cut the welfare **state**. Then every man, woman, and child shall **elate**.

"Let this be your **fate**! Move us through the White House **gate**!

"Now--if I weren't running **late** for another **date**, a dinner of $100 a **plate**, most gladly I'd stay and **debate**."

☞ See *Story 27*

Story 55

Wait On and Weight Off

There is:
The **wait** on the tables
The **wait** in the lines, and
The **weight** off the dieters

There is:
The sea **strait**, and
The dire **straits**

There is:
The **straight** line
The **straight** flush
The **straight** ahead
The **straight** answer
The **straight** character &
The character **trait**

There is:
The eating **plate**
The license **plate**
The name **plate**
The head **plate**
The hair **plait**

There is:
The fishing **bait**
The nagging **bait**
The hounding **bait**
The teasing **bait**

And there is:
The girl **ate**, and
The boy **eight**

Story 56

Scathed

Derrick got badly **scathed,**
Cut by the blade of a **lathe.**
So in i-o-dine his finger had to be **bathed,**
Then of course in a bandage **swathed,**
Then later **unswathed,**
But unhealed, **reswathed,**
Then, finally, fully healed, once more **unswathed.**

☞ See Story 29

Story 57

The Brave

Little Hawk was an Indian **brave** who did not like the way the White Man did **behave**. So with tomahawk, he **gave wave** after **wave** of settler a close **shave**.

Save for their scalps, he buried them in a mass **grave** within a mountain **cave**. Now this **gave** White Man his reason to **rave**.

Story 58

Really Fazed

When the barn of **Farmer Hayes** went **ablaze**, he stood in a **daze**, eyes **glazed**, watching the structure being **razed**.

Luckily his animals were out to **graze**, for in the smoky **haze** their stalls would've been a **maze**. Nevertheless, **Hayes** became **crazed**. From then on he would only blankly **gaze**.

Story 59

Praise The Lord

While riding in a horse-drawn **chaise** the minister **prays** for words to put into proper **phrase**, which will give the Lord due **praise**.

He hopes to **upraise** those wayward **strays** who are in a sinful **phase** and might e-ter-nal-ly **braise**.

AR

Story 60

The Bizarre Czar

In Russia there once lived a **czar** who traveled the roads of **tar** drinking booze from a **jar**. He hit every **bar**, both near and **far**, looking for someone to box or **spar**.

So often he wrecked his **car** that it had several dents, a long **scar**, and a door that sat a**jar**.

But what else should be expected from this **czar**, who on **par** got so drunk all he saw were **stars** and believed he lived on the planet **Mars**?

☞ See *Story 74*

Story 61

Catch The Barbs

There is a fishhook **barb**
There is a clothes **garb**
There is a girl, **Darb**
There is another girl, **Barb**

There is smelly **garb**
There is a fence wire **barb**
There is a witty and
an insulting **barb** &
There is a vi-cious &
a de-li-cious **rhubarb**

Story 62

March to the Golden Arch

When it is hot,
People should sit under a shady **larch**.
And when it is very hot,
People should **march**
To McDonald's Golden **Arch**
Why?
To drink cold drinks so their throats won't **parch**.

☞ See Story 66

Story 63

Larded With "Ards"

There is:
The National **Guard**
The football **guard**
The prison **guard**
And the face **guard**

There is:
The jail **yard**
The back **yard**
The railroad **yard**
And the measuring **yard**

There is:
The fat or **lard** and
The poet or **bard**

There is:
The playing **card**
The membership **card**
The score **card**
And the human **card**

And there is:
The **hard** rock
The **hard** problem
The **hard** look and
The **hard** fact

Story 64

Arf, Arf

The shaggy dog (cer-tain-ly no **dwarf**)
Lives with his master upon a **wharf**
Whenever hungry, he barks, "**ARF, ARF**"
Then fish is served him which down he'll **SCARF**
Up
Yet not once has he thrown Up
In other words--
B
A
R
F!

Story 65

Sarge and Marge

Father and daughter are **Sarge** and **Marge**.

In combat, **Sarge** leads his soldiers on an enemy **charge,** with weapons loaded with gunpowder **charge**. And on base he runs a river **barge**.

The duties of young **Marge** are not so **large**: housework is her only assigned **charge**. Therefore she plays tiddlywinks to give herself a "second **charge**."

Story 66

Noah's Ark

To whom did Noah **hark** before he built his **ark**?

Did he work just in the sunlight or also in the **dark**? Did he take any birds like a robin or a **lark**? Of course he didn't take a whale nor a **shark**! But did he take two seals, and loudly did they **bark**?

What does the Bible **remark**? Does it tell of the voyage on the world's **arc**, the flood's high-water **mark**, and where the **ark** finally came to **park**?

For how long did the earth look **stark**? When did Noah's problems no longer **cark**?

☞ See *Story 62*

Story 67

A Quarrel

Carl,
Blamed for causing the traffic to **snarl**,
Got into a **quarrel**.
With lips **gnarled**,
Carl snarled.
Had there not been
A policeman mounted on a **sorrel**[1]
There likely would have been
More than a mere **quarrel**.

1) A reddish-brown horse.

Story 68

Farming

If you have a strong **arm**,
A gun to protect yourself from **harm**
And if work causes you no **alarm**
Then life on a **farm** is but a **charm**.

Story 69

A True Yarn

The Scots call a mountain lake a **tarn**. They call a stone landmark a **cairn**. Although peculiar, the Scots call both an animal house and a youngster a **barn**. Be that as it may, the sheep in their **barn** provide the best **darn yarn** that any tailor should ever hope to **darn**.

Story 70

The Jew's Harp

Although José enjoyed playing his **Jew's Harp**, he downright hated the upright **harp**.

Consequently his mother would **harp** (He called it "**carp.**"), "Play your **harp**! Play your **harp**!"

But José preferred to fish for **carp**. So he did so, while thumbing tunes in **A-sharp** upon his oral **harp**.

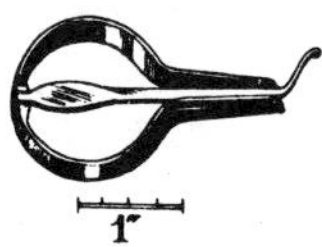

Jew's-harp

Story 71

Is School A Farce?

Dolores's brains were rather few or **sparse**. Simple sentences she could not **parse**. Nor could she tell a horse from an **arse**.

What's more, she thought that school was one big, hi-lar-i-ous **farce**!

Story 72

Art Can Make You Smart

When you're young it is best to study **art**. To be successful, you must take an active **part** and give it all your **heart**.

You might **start** by drawing an arrow or a **dart**, a wagon or a **cart**, a doe or a **hart**, or even a pop **tart**.

It is fun to study **art**, but what is more important--**art** can make you **smart**.

Story 73

Marv and Harve

BUTCHER

Marv
and
Harve
will
never
starve
because
Marv
and
Harve
are
woodworker
and
butcher
re-spec-tive-ly
who
so
ex-pert-ly--
carve

WOODWORKER / LUMBERJACK

ĀR̃

Story 74

The Hare And The Mare

"I don't easily **scare**," said the **hare**, "except perhaps in a **snare**."

The **mare** replied, "**Hare**, I wouldn't ever purposely **scare**. It's just that my sight is **impaired**, giving the false im-pres-sion that I **stare**."

"Oh, of this I wasn't **aware**!" com-ment-ed the **Hare**. "Do let our friend-ship **repair**!"

"Sure thing!" said the **mare**. "And for showing me you **care**, I offer you a ride on my back **bare**, for which **there** shan't be any **fare**!"

☞ See *Story 60*

Story 75

Beware of Bear

Cher said, "I shouldn't **swear**, but these woods do **scare** me so, **Pierre**.

"The woods have made my patience **wear**, and now **they're** more than I can **scarcely bear**. You should have taken more **care**! You know I am a **mil-lion-aire** and want to live to be a **forebear**; that is, to **bear** a child who'll be my **heir**.

"Never again will I **err** and **dare** go **anywhere** near **where there** are any **bear**."

☞ See *Story 129*

Story 76

Love at the County Fair

At the **fair** I watched a **pair** of grizzly **bear** that had been caught asleep in **their lair**.

To my surprise, they ob-vi-ous-ly thought **their** life was not **unfair**. They received ex-cel-lent **care**. Moreover, they had a better-than--ever love **affair**, and a **flair** for swinging through the **air** without feeling the slightest **scare**.

Ĕ

Story 77

The Deb's Web

Jeb
A Southern **Reb**[1]
At his lowest **ebb**
Got caught by a conniving **deb**[2]
She had said their dating was just for fun
Then she said she wanted to bear his son
So tenderly trapped in her **web**
He married her in the month of **Feb**

1) Rebel, a young man.
2) Debutante, a young well-off woman.

Story 78

Rebecca

Rebecca cried, "My clothes make me look a **wreck**. All of them are spotted with lint **specks**. And I look so fat in **checks**!"

Her husband, hearing her **beck**, gave her a **peck** on her **neck** and said, "Dear, **trek** to the store and buy whatever in the **heck** you **reck** will make you the prettiest **Czech** in all **Quebec**."

Story 79

A Collection

Affect, the outcome

Collect sea shells

Recollect the facts

Correct the answer

Connect the dots

Disconnect the phone

Deflect the ball

Defect, the fault

Detect the mistake

Dissect the frog

Direct the play

Elect the candidate

Re-elect the senator

Erect the building

Effect, the outcome

Expect the best

Eject the pilot

Reject the plan

Sect, the holy order

Insect, the bug

Intersect the lines

Inspect the goods

Infect the cut

Disinfect the cut

Inflect the voice

Inject the needle

Neglect the duty

Project the line

Perfect the invention

Protect the helpless

Reflect the light

Respect the police

Select the choicest

Suspect, the defendant

Dialect, the language

Intellect, the brain &

Architect, the builder

Story 80

Not a Shred of Sense

Ned and **Fred pled** with their mom to use their **sled**.

Their mother replied, "But the ice is hard. And if you fall, it will feel like **lead**. Besides, isn't it too slippery for the **thoroughbred**? Nevertheless, if you insist, go **ahead**. But I **dread** something tragic lies **ahead**."

They **led** the horse to the bridle **shed** and hitched her to the **sled**. Then they jumped aboard and at top speed **sped** across their snowy **homestead**.

As you may have guessed, both boys ended up nearly **dead**. **Ned** had a cracked **head**; and **Fred**, cuts that profusely **bled**.

☞ See *Story 107*

Story 81

The Winning Edge

To be on the winning **edge**
Gain some **knowledge**
Make this your **pledge**
And hold ig-no-rance as **sac-ri-lege**

Story 82

Theft Doesn't Pay

Being **bereft** of what is right, **Mr. Peff** turned to the **left**, to **theft**. He stole sweaters stitched in **weft**.

The able police traced the tracks which behind he **left** where they found **Peff** in pos-ses-sion of the goods marked with the code letter "**F**."

Story 83

Crazy Meg

Please, **Craig**
Please, **Peg**,
Begged Meg
I'm not the **Black Plague**
I'm not a worthless **dreg**
So please don't call me "**NUT . . . Meg**"
Now let's drink from my **keg**
Beer enough to fill a **leg**

Story 84

A Life That Jells

Farmer **Ra-pha-el dwells** in the **dell** with his beautiful **belle, Jez-e-bel.**

Every morning **Raphael** arises at six when he hears the **knell** of the cow **bell**. Then he milks his bovine 'til his buckets **swell**. Afterwards he may **fell** a few trees, or gather honey from honeycomb **cells.**

Jezebel grows **bluebells** and she gathers **sea shells** that she **sells** in **Carmel**.

The life they live is **swell**. He never has a **fell** look, and she never a foul word. And each wishes the other **well**, which is a wish made weekly at their wishing **well**.

Story 85

Our Creator's Realm

Of everything that ever was, is, and ever will be--God rules at the **helm**. Within his **realm** is every oak and every **elm**. He has made the oceans **whelm** and the mountains *belch*. He has made all people: the Irish, the Scotch, and the *Welch*.

He has imbued man with the intellect to gather oil from the con-ti-nen-tal **shelf**, to dream up the little **elf**, and in other ways to amuse **himself**. He has made each one of us in such a way that as a young **whelp** we **yelp** for our loving mother's **help**.

Most important, He gave us His Ten Commandments to be **upheld**, in the hope that His and our will will **meld**.

Story 86

Badly Belted

Despite the snow that had not yet begun to **melt**, they came from all over the farm **belt**. Many **svelte** ladies came wearing a fur **pelt**, escorted by gentle-men bundled in **felt**. They came out to see the boxing bout between Louis, the challenger, and Braddock, the champ.

Everyone **felt** it would be a good fight; however, Louis **welted** and **pelted** the champ with more **belts** than he had heretofore ever been **dealt**.

Soon Braddock was on the canvas, where on one knee he **knelt**, as he **dwelt** on flowers and how sweet they **smelt**.

Story 87

Bad For Her Health

"Lonnie," said her mommy, "any more cookies would be bad for your **health**. Besides, we should preserve the cookie **wealth**, thus I shall **shelve** the other **twelve**."

But at her first chance, Lonnie used **stealth**, taking one after another through the **twelfth**.

"Daughter," said her father later, "you were told not to **delve** into the cookies your mother **shelved**. Therefore you shall have a couple of whacks with the **helve** of my ax for each taken of the **twelve**."

Story 88

To The Heavenly Diadem

The world is full of **mayhem**
You wonder, What is the **stem**?
Perhaps our lust for a **gem**,
Greed to have more than "**Them**"
Or belief--
We're better than **Clem**
Maybe we ought not to **contemn**
Or to **condemn**
But pray to the **diadem**
For grace at our **requiem**

Story 89

Tempted

The devil may **attempt** to **tempt**
Even those who hold sin in **contempt**
In other words no soul is **exempt**
For Satan may come even in a dream **dreamt**

Story 90

The Fox's Ken

The sly fox cannot always catch the flighty **wren**, so now and **then** he must satisfy his **yen** for fowl with a plump **hen**.

He has the **ken** to wait till **ten**, **when** fast asleep are all the **men**. **Then** he leaves his mountain **den**, and comes down through the **glen**. **When** all is clear, he steals into the chicken **pen**, clenches his teeth around a **hen**, and takes off just as fast as he possibly **can**.

Story 91

Incensed

"You're a bit **dense**!" one knight said to another. This caused the latter to take **offense**, actually he was **incensed**. He bellowed out, "My honor needs **defense**!"

As the fight was about to **commence**, the former got **tense**. He pled, "What I said was utter **nonsense**, not making a lick of **sense**. Please, won't you excuse my **impertinence**?"

The latter answered, "Now that's showing better **sense**, but another slight to my **intelligence** will spell blood as your grave, grave **consequence**."

Story 92

The Comely Wench

Once upon a time a young boy fell for a comely **French wench**. Her dev-as-ta-ting beauty made him **blench**. For days on end he dreamt of nothing but having her in his **clench**, in the park, on a **bench**. He thought he'd never **quench** his thirst for this beautiful **wench**.

Be that as it may, when he nearly had her in his **clench**, he fell plumb backwards off the **bench**, repelled by the cheapest, rankest perfume **stench**.

Story 93

We Depend On Mom

There are many affairs to which mother has to **attend**, because she has many children for whom to **fend**. In the day, she works in a big store in **South Bend**. Her job is to **vend** clothes of the fashionable **trend**. And some nights she must bar **tend**.

When she returns home, she has to **spend** time with each child who wants to **bend** her ear. She also has to **mend** socks, perhaps **send** a letter, and always **lend** a hand to fix a meal.

Thanks to Mom, who is our *bestest* **friend** and whom we highly **commend**, we all should **ascend** to great heights in the **end**.

Story 94

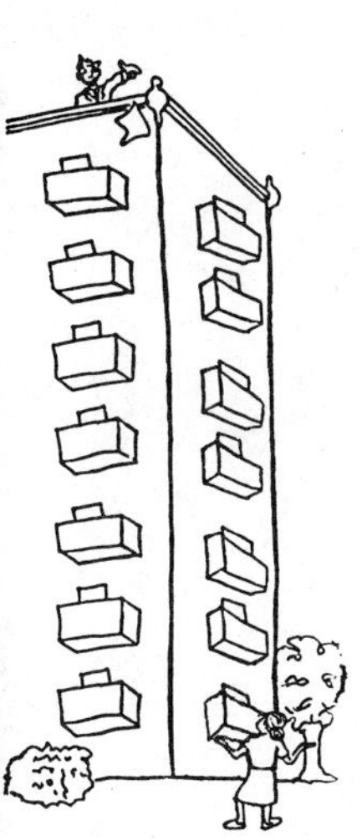

Pent Up

Once upon a time in the city of **Trent**, there lived an elderly **gent** by the name of **Ghent**. Being **pent** up in a **pent-house**, **Mr. Ghent** be came **dis-con-tent**. So one day he **sent** his final **payment** to the **resi-dent** manager, **Mrs. Kent**. In-cluded was a note in which he said he had no **in-tent** to pay the next month's "sky-high **rent**" and soon to expect his **de-scent**, by which he **meant** good-bye to **Mrs. Kent**.

So **Mr. Ghent**, who always had the **bent** to live in wilderness **wonder-ment**, **went** off into the woods where his final days were **spent** quite **content**, sniffing animal **scent**, living in a pup **tent**.

Story 95

As The Lion Leapt

Through the fields the safari **swept**
Until we came upon a lion that **slept**.
Silently we **crept**,
But the beast awoke:
Our passage, it wouldn't **accept**,
We were ter-ri-bly **inept**
And instantly **wept**;
That is, all **except**
Our guide who **kept**
A **lariat**
With which to make an **adept**
Intercept
Of the lion as it **leapt**.

Story 96

A Financial Mess

"**Yes**, Ma'am," I **confess**, "**Bess** and I gambled playing **chess**. It was fun, more or **less**.

"We were playing like money was hot off the **press**! Though, truly, it was utterly **fortuneless**. **Bess**, she was **merciless**. She left me not only **penniless**, but **clothesless**, for she took all my money and my brand-new **dress**."

Story 97

Thresh These Over

There is:

The human **flesh**
The fruity **flesh**
The thrashing **thresh**
The splashing **thresh**
The grating **mesh**
The fencing **mesh**
The dewy **fresh**
The tasty **fresh**
The naughty **fresh**
And the earthy **creche**

Story 98

A Grand Quest $

Roy Rogers was the **best** cowboy in all the **West**. He did his job with **zest**, but never killed in **jest**. Some say he was **blest** to win every shootout **contest**, while others claim he wore a bullet-proof **vest**.

Whatever the case, no one was able to **wrest** Roy from Hollywood's **crest**.

Today he has even a greater **quest**. As you know, his restaurants have a million **guests**, spending millions of dollars on Double-R-burgers and chicken **breasts**.

Story 99

Brett's All Wet

"Don't **fret**, **Claudette**," said **Brett**. "My pretty **brunette pet**, there's nothing to **sweat**, for there's not any **threat**. I know we're entangled in a financial **net**, **beset** by creditors. But somehow, some way, someone will help us **get** out of **debt**.

"Then, when all our bills have been **met** and we are securely **set**, I'll **let** you buy anything and everything: perhaps a **Corvette**, or even a personal **jet**. So, dear, **let** your dreams **whet**."

Claudette responded, "The only thing **wet** is you, **Brett**. And **Brett**, you are all **wet**, soaking **wet**!"

Story 100

Make A Good Catch

If you were a bucket, spring water you'd **fetch**
If you were an arrow, feathers you'd **fletch**
If you were a river, a canyon you'd **etch**
If you were a pen, a drawing you'd **sketch**
If you were rubber, greatly you'd **s-t-r-e-t-c-h**
But since you're merely you--
Make a good **catch**, and marry no **wretch**.

Story 101

After Abel's Death

After Cain caused Abel's **death**, once again God instilled His Heavenly **breath**, blessing Adam and Eve with **Seth**.

Seth married Enosh and they begot others, who begot others, among them **Japeth** and **Mary Beth**. They married and begot others, who begot others, who eventually begot us--who **continueth** begetting through this century, the **twentieth**.

☞ See *Stories 125 & 126*

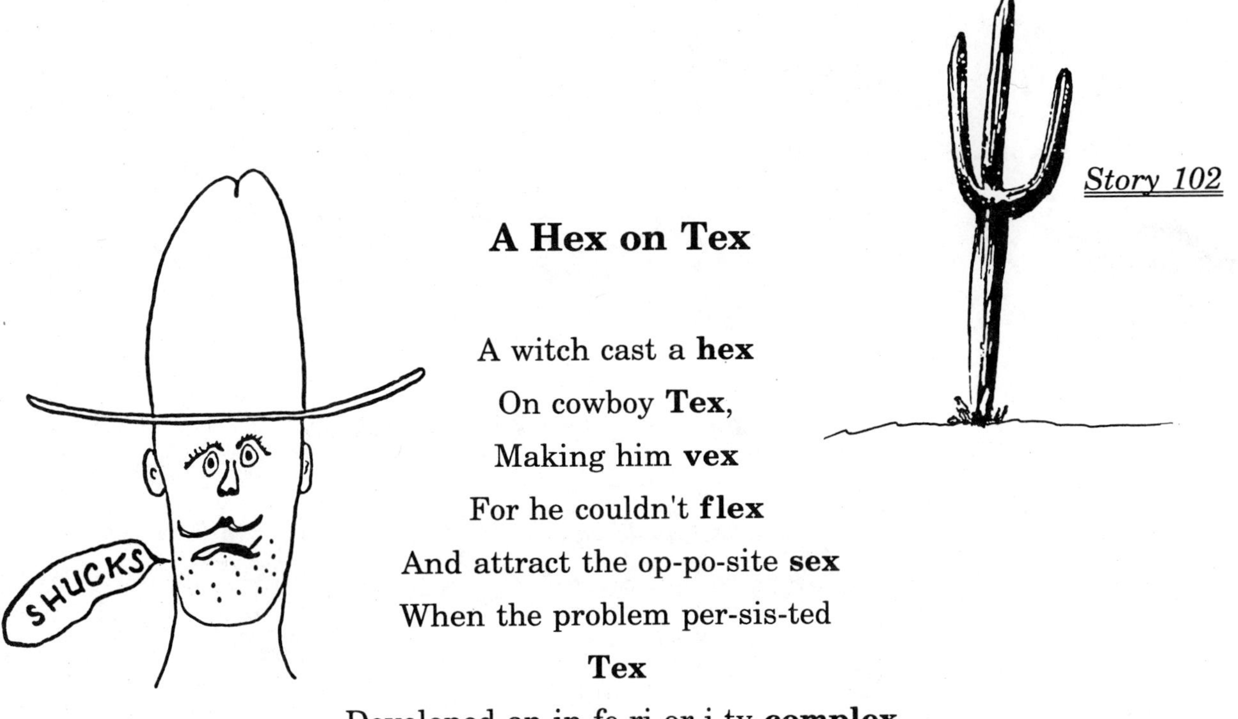

Story 102

A Hex on Tex

A witch cast a **hex**
On cowboy **Tex**,
Making him **vex**
For he couldn't **flex**
And attract the op-po-site **sex**
When the problem per-sis-ted
Tex
Developed an in-fe-ri-or-i-ty **complex**

Ē

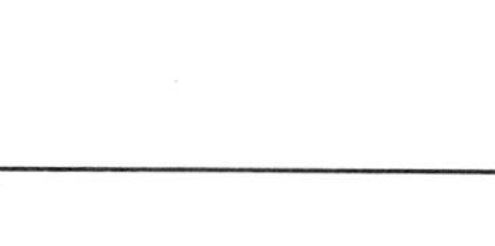

Story 103

Teed Off

Lee, **Rosalie**, and **Marie** joined **me** at **three** on the first golf **tee**.

We were feeling fancy **free** and full of **glee**. But things soon changed when a **bumblebee** came out of a **tree**. My friends were quick to **flee**, but it caught slow **me** with a stinger on the **knee**.

Gee I was **angry!** so much so that the management would **agree** to forego the green **fee**, and let **me** play **free**.

Story 104

Bugged by a Flea

Near the **sea** I sat on a grassy **lea**
As **happy** as could **be**
Until a **pesky flea**
Started to bother **me**
Despite my earnest **plea**
He ate my last green **pea**
And drank all my **Lipton Tea**

Story 105

Impeached

Joan and Bill walked to the woods' far **reaches**, where they climbed some tall **beeches**. But when they came down they found in their **breeches** blood-sucking **leeches**. So they ran home making blood-curdling **screeches**.

Their mother said, "I will not make a **speech**, nor will I **preach**. But I hope that this will **teach** you **each** that a promise you do not **breach**. You promised to pick only **peaches**, but instead you climbed those high forbidden **beeches**.

"Now that your promise has been **breached**, your total character is therefore **impeached**."

Story 106

The Prayerful Swede

The **Swede**, dressed in his best **tweed**, mounted his **steed** and galloped off at **exceedingly** fast **speed**. He was late for church in **Runnymede**.

In church, he said the Apostles' **Creed**, promised not to sin by **greed**, and prayed for the souls in purgatory to be **freed**. He prayed to **heed** God's word and to do a daily good **deed**, especially by helping those in **need**.

Finally he prayed that his business *would* **succeed** and that his hairline *wouldn't* **recede**.

Story 107

All I Need

I pray on my rosary **bead**
For an upright life to **lead**
For nothing else do I **plead**
For nothing else do I **need**
Except the knowledge to **read**
And pro-nounce such words as **knead**,
supersede, and **millipede**

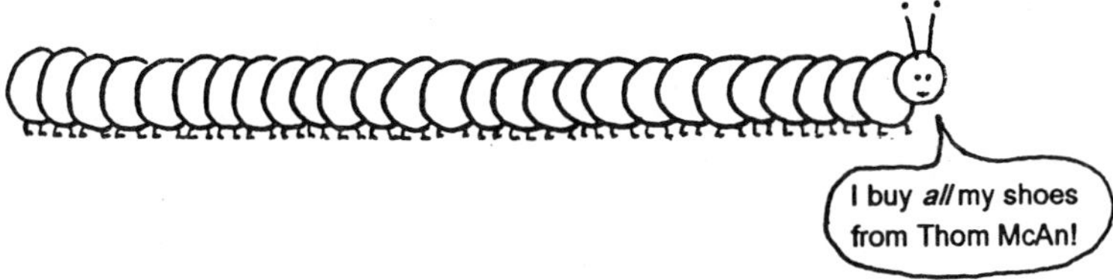
I buy *all* my shoes from Thom McAn!

☞ See *Story 80*

Story 108

Ed

In League

Ed and Fred enjoyed crime's **intrigue**. But as time passed, Fred told his **colleague**, "This work is causing me **fatigue**. Thus I must **renege**!"

Upon hearing this, Ed shot Fred dead, then dropped his former **colleague** down to the deepest sea **league**.

Fred

Story 109

The Horse Thief

"I'll be **brief**," said Big Bull, the Sioux Indian **chief**. "It's my firm **belief** that we must scalp the horse **thief**. He steals our ponies and sells them as **beef**.

"He has brought us nothing but **grief**. He will never turn over a new **leaf**, so only his death will spell **relief**."

Story 110

No More Leeks

Zeke, the **Greek**, worked for an Arabian **sheik**. He managed to **eke** out a **meek** existence selling onions called **leeks**.

Working this job **week** in and **week** out made his clothes **reek**.

As time went by his stink stunk so much his **sleek**, **chic Monique** would angrily **shriek**. She refused to give him so much as a kiss on his **cheek**. Ter-ri-bly disturbed, he threw his clothes into a **creek** and told the **sheik**--a new job he would **seek**!

Story 111

A Bird Unique

On a hilly **peak**
Along the **Chesapeake**
Lives a bird **unique.**
Like a parrot, he can **speak**
But his call is a **shriek**
That breaks into a **squeak**.
He possesses a huge **beak**,
Plumage, white with an orange **streak.**
And he has a bulbous **physique**.
What's more, he's so **weak**
That flying makes his bones **creak**

Story 112

Miss Beale

Miss Beale jumped into her **keel** with her rod 'n' **reel** and said to herself, "Oh how lucky I **feel**. Maybe today I'll catch a shark or **seal**."

But as hard as she fished and as hard as she wished, all she could catch was a boot **heel** and a slimy **eel**.

Story 113

O'Neil's Spiel

For the good of the **commonweal**
I make this earnest **appeal**
To strike up a workable **deal**--
One that is just, not **unreal**,
One that shall make our e-con-o-my **heal**
All taxes we shall **repeal**
Except for one **we'll** double on steak and **veal**.
On this proposal we should place our state **seal**,
Doing it with utmost **zeal**.
Now let's let the bells ring out a joyous **peal**!

Story 114

On The Battlefield

Far from **Chesterfield**, upon the barren **weald** was the knights' chosen **battlefield**.

They would fight to avenge sores that for years remained **unhealed**. They dressed in armor **shield** bandying swords they would skillfully **wield**.

As one advanced, the other **reeled**. Neither would **yield**. So back and forth it went 'til one finally **keeled**.

Story 115

Steamed

The early morning sun rose, finding **Rasheem** sitting upon a wooden **beam**. As water for coffee began to **steam**, he heard a loud **scream**! He wondered, "Was **Shaakeem** having a bad **dream**?" No! While washing she had fallen into the **stream**.

This made him laugh and laugh 'til he nearly burst at the **seam**. But to **Shaakeem** it didn't **seem** like such a "**scream**." She thought he was **mean** and said, "**Rasheem**, this **seems** like the end of our mar-ri-age **dream**."

Story 116

The Wrong Theme

Eileen declared, "Writing a **theme seems** a bit **extreme**. My effort would need be **supreme**. First I'd have to devise a **scheme**, then da dat . . . da dat . . . da dat. Soon problems would **teem**, my brain would **steam**, and I'd likely **scream**. So instead of writing a difficult **theme**, I think I'll hum my carefree **theme,** fishing for **bream** in a mountain **stream**."

Ironic as it *does* **seem**, **Eileen**, who previously didn't **deem** highly of **academe**, got an "F" which devastated her **self-esteem**.

Story 117

Our College Dean

Ms. Green, our student **dean**, possessed a fore-bod-ing **mien** like that of a combat **marine**.

She wouldn't allow us to wear blue **jeans** nor to read any **magazines**. Of course, there wasn't a **canteen**! She even pro-hib-i-ted tea and coke citing **caffeine**. Five days a week she had the caf-e-te-ri-a serve us baked **beans** and collard **greens**.

She claimed she wanted us **lean**; however, she suc-ceed-ed only in being awfully **mean**.

Story 118

The Queen

Queen Josephine, only **nineteen**, is by far the most beautiful woman her kingdom has ever **seen**.

She is always **serene**, with the most pleasing **mien**. She never vents her **spleen** nor acts the slightest bit **mean**. She is tall and **lean**. Her eyes are emerald **green**. Her face is cover-girl **clean**, and her hair shines with lustrous **sheen**.

Her sense of dress is so **keen** that nearly an hour it takes her to **preen**. But she always makes the most de-light-ful **scene**, es-pe-cial-ly with King **Constantine**.

Story 119

Little Bo Peep

Little Bo Peep worked so hard for her **keep**, because her master was cruel and **cheap**.

All day long she had to **sweep**. At night she had to tend her **sheep**. **Miss Bo Peep** would never have gotten any **sleep** had it not been for a few birds who knew to **cheep** whenever they heard the Big Bad Wolf **creep**.

Over time her sorrow became so **deep** that she nearly drowned **steeped** in her tears that wouldn't **seep**.

Story 120

The Jeep

On such a good bargain he made a quick **leap**

To buy what he thought was a beautiful **jeep**

But oh my goodness what a terrible **heap**!

As hard as she tried she could scarcely **creep**

So lickety-split he resold her quite **cheap**

Still--a profit he managed to **reap**

<u>*Story 121*</u>

The Reeses

Old man **Reese** lived with his little **niece**, **Bernice**, outside of **Nice**.

On their farm (that had a 99-year **lease**), they raised a few **geese**. They also raised sheep for their beautiful **fleece**, which they sold to the best tailors of **Greece** to make pants that never lose their **crease**.

Year in and year out their hard work did not **cease**, but the hard work made their profits **increase** and their worries **decrease**.

Therefore the two were able to live in **peace** until that final day on which **Mr. Reese** finally did **decease**.

☞ See *Story 128*

<u>*Story 122*</u>

The East

I have been to the North, South, West, and **East**
And it is the **East** that I like the **least**
There their **priests** hold sacred the four-legged **beast**
Therefore chicken with rice and bread with **yeast**
Is their one and only singular **feast**

Story 123

A Special Treat

For ac-com-plish-ing your ac-a-dem-ic **feat**
You have won yourself a special **treat**.
Would you like a drink to **beat** the **heat**?
Perhaps a tasty cut of **meat**?
If there's nothing you want to **eat**,
How about a Yankees' grandstand **seat**?
Wouldn't that be super **neat**?
I **repeat**--Wouldn't that be super **neat**?

Story 124

A Proper Greeting

Regardless whether it's raining a **sheet** of **sleet**
Or for some other reason you'd like to be **fleet**,
Whenever you **meet** friend or stranger on the **street**,
Be as **sweet** as a sugar **beet**,
Greet him with words **upbeat**
And smile, be it **Pete** or **Marguerite**.

Story 125

Calculating Keith

Keith
Picked up his scythe by its **sneath**,
To shear some sprigs to make a **wreath**
To begift his dying **Aunt Lolith**
Hoping that this slick trick
Would pull him out from **beneath**
His debts
And out of Edinburg's ghetto of **Leith**
With the cash she'd soon **be-queath**

☞ See *Story 101*

Story 126

Seething

If per chance a doctor were to **unsheathe**
A scalpel[1] to help some little baby **teethe**,
Do you think its mother would anx-ious-ly **breathe**?
Do you think she might an-gri-ly **seethe**?
And, in court, do you think he'd wor-ried-ly grieve?

1) A surgical knife.

☞ See *Story 101*

Story 127

Sailing With Steve

Eve, by noon tomorrow we shall **leave**
In a sailboat owned by **Steve**
The weather should be good, I **believe**.
Figure 8s and Ss we shall **weave**.
Through the dangerous shoals we shall **reeve**
But I'll be certain to be home by **eve**.
Otherwise, my dearest **Eve**, you'll **peeve**
And I, con-se-quent-ly, shall **grieve**.

Story 128

Learn These

Bees, the honeymakers
Breeze, the wind
Breeze, the cinch
Fees, the expense
He's the man
Louise, the girl
Peas, the vegetable
Pleas, the requests
Seize the prey
Seize the problem
Sees the answer
Seas, the water
Freeze the water
Frieze, the art work
Grease the pan
Grease the squeak

Squeeze the lemon
Squeeze the profits
Sneeze, the cold
Sneeze, the scoff
Tees the ball
Teas, the drinks
Tease the hair
Tease the boys
Ease the pain
Ease the punishment
Wheeze, the sound
Wheeze, the joke
And **she's**--well
She's the **sleaze**

☞ See *Story 121*

ĒR̃

Story 129

The Deer Hunters

When Bill went to hunt for **deer**
With Joe, his buddy and **peer**,
Bill's wife gave him a scornful **fleer**
And declared with a nasty **sneer**,
"How can you two shoot a **deer**?"
Then her eyes began to **tear**.
Nevertheless, the men grabbed their hunting **gear**.

Down the road some they stopped for **beer**.
Now **beer** is excellent for good **cheer**
But it may make your vision **blear**,
And also make your judgment **veer**,
Thus altering the way things **appear**.

In light of this, it's not so **queer**
To mistake a cow for a **deer**.
So when Joe shot the farmer's **steer**
That angry man made it quite **clear**
By shouting loudly in their **ear**
That if they so much as go **near**
His homestead the following **year**
He'd make their scalps his **souvenir**.

☞ See *Story 75*

Story 130

Pierce

The swords-man was **fierce**, with an ex-cel-lent **tierce**[1]. Any of-fense to him, even the **merest**, in-tend-ed or not, had his op-ponents always in tears, shaken by fears, knowing likely he'd slash off their ears.

And after each duel, the cruel **Pierce** was wont to celebrate im-bi-bing wine straight from a **tierce**.

1. A parry stroke; also a cask or keg.

Story 131

As His Number Neared

As his draft number **neared** the more cowardly he **appeared**. His eyes con-tin-u-ous-ly **teared**, so much they besoaked his **beard**. He **feared** that for war he could never con-sci-en-tious-ly be **geared**.

Friends warned him that if he fled to Canada, his good name would be **smeared**, and that people would say he's a little bit **weird**.

Nevertheless, with vision **bleared**, he deserted 'til the smoke in Viet Nam **cleared**.

Ȓ

Story 132

What's Causing The Stir?

"**Sir**, can you tell me what **spurs** the squirrels to **stir**? I've never seen them so busily **whir**. They're like a **blur**. Nor have I heard them so noisily **chirr**. They jump about the oaks and **firs** as though their coats have thistles and **burs**."

The man replied to **her**, "Does it not **occur** to you that you can no longer hear a cat **purr**? Don't you know that there is a high price on **fur**, even the **fur** of a **cur**? Now **answer**, What *should* a squirrel **infer** seeing your coat of rabbit **fur**?"

☞ See Stories *201, 351*

Story 133

Herbal Tea

Miss Lee couldn't **curb** her yearning for this tea, a tea **superb** as says the **blurb**. And because her stomach is easy to **disturb** as is her smile to **perturb**, to buy it **Herb** would travel to the city from miles beyond the **suburb**, somewhere in the **exurb**.

But **Herb**, who tired of traveling, now grows the **herb** between his sidewalk and the county **curb**.

Story 134

So L-O-N-G In Church

In St. Paul, at St. Peter's Catholic Church, Father Patrick, the head priest, preached from his **perch**--a pulpit of pine, poplar, and paper **birch**.

He said a couple re-dun-dant and rep-e-ti-tious, though re-mark-a-bly and ri-dic-u-lous-ly re-mem-ber-a-ble things:

"Each and every single sol-i-ta-ry sinner's soul has been **besmirched** with stain, smear, smudge, or **smirch**. Therefore, every month on the first, fifth, fifteenth, and twenty-fifth, and on the first and fifth Fridays, we ought not in the least feast, but fast . . . from fish like flounder, pike, pickerel, and **perch**.

"The Bible we must **research**, **searching**, scouting, striving for our Heavenly plot . . . our place, our **perch**. Otherwise we leave to chance being left alone, lorn, forlorn, lonely in a **lurch**."

Story 135

"The Nerd"

Mark **Byrd** didn't know the sound **heard** from the sheep **herd**. As a matter of fact he couldn't spell a single **word**.

He didn't know that milk has wheys and **curd**. He couldn't even tell a plane from a **bird**, nor first base from **third**.

Con-se-quent-ly, his classmates would call him "The **Nerd**." And now, today, **Byrd** is a farmhand picking up **turd**.

Story 136

Murph

In the 12th cen-tu-ry England
There lived a man whose name was **Murph**
Now just because he was a **serf**
His highness the king called him "**scurf** "
Which was wrong
For all day long
He fished the seas riding the **surf**
Or plowed the fields tilling the **turf**.

Story 137

The Deadliest Scourge

Dressed in dark **serge**, family and friends **converged** at church to pray that the soul of the dearly departed be **purged**. They **immerged** into silent prayer. And when they **emerged**, they were **urged** to gen-er-ous-ly **splurge** to fight cancer, the deadliest **scourge**.

Then as the choir chanted a doleful **dirge**, a **surge** of sorrow swept the mourners to crying's **verge**.

Story 138

Failure Lurks

Hahmon is a **Turk** who came to the States and found **work** as a stock **clerk**. But over time he began to **shirk** his **work**--which made his boss **irk**.

So Hahmon took another job as a soda **jerk**. But again his interest didn't **perk**, and he greeted his customers with a sassy **smirk**.

His new boss said, "Hahmon, you have a most dis-a-gree-a-ble **quirk**. You make the clearest day seem as gloomy as **murk**. Therefore you'd best look for other **work**."

Hahmon replied, "I care not, **Mr. Burke**. Being a **jerk** is certainly no job for this in-tel-li-gent **Turk**!"

Story 139

The Earl and Cheryl

Merrill was a well-mannered English **earl**.

One morning as he drew his drapes into **furls**, he saw through his window the most beautiful **girl** with golden cas-cad-ing **curls**. At once his head began to **whirl** as he saw buttercups, gol-den-rods, and mar-i-golds--all in a **swirling whorl**. Right then he knew he'd give the single life a **hurl** and marry the love-ly **Cheryl**.

And when she said yes, the thankful **earl** kissed the sweet **girl** and promised her the **world**.

Story 140

The Life of the Worm

Being that the bird is unafraid of any **germ**, all day long it pecks the **berm** looking for the **worm**.

Unfortunately for the **worm**, no matter how des-per-ate-ly it may **squirm**, it cannot escape the beak in which it's held so **firm**. This is why the life of the **worm** is but a short, short **term**.

Story 141

"Really! Mr. Byrne"

In the Swiss capital of **Bern** there is a pretty miss named **Fern**. She lives with her dad, **Mr. Byrne**, who is nice but a bit **stern**.

He says, "**Fern**, on the subject of marriage, I care not how much you **yearn**. There are many worthless suitors whom you must **spurn**.

"You don't want one as flighty as an **ern** or a **tern**. You must find one who can **discern** right from wrong, left from right, and up from down.

"Ideally, he should be well-**learned**--perhaps a doctor or a young **intern**. He should be willing to **churn** his mind to **earn** a buck, and to bank that buck to bring about a big **return**. In other words, he must be willing to fill your **fern** and flower **urn** with oodles and oodles of money to **burn**.

Story 142

The Twerp

In **Antwerp** there lives a boy named **Erp** whom everyone calls a **twerp**.

He throws stones at little birds whenever they **chirp**. And during meals he will loudly **slurp**, then laugh and pardon himself with an even louder **burp**.

Story 143

The Busy Nurse

There once was a busy **nurse**. With every patient she would pa-tient-ly **converse**. Her remarks were always **terse**, though pleasing and often in **verse**. There was nothing to which she was **averse** to help make a patient's condition **reverse**.

But now and again a patient would turn for the **worse**. Then **first** she'd call the patient's family citing the **curse**, and next the morgue requesting its **hearse**.

Story 144

Boys! Stay Alert!

Little boys should stay **alert**: on guard against little girls who like to **flirt**, especially those that are saucy or **pert**.

At first they may say you're sweeter than **dessert**, or that they like your spiffy **shirt**. But when they get angry you'll be **hurt**. In a **spurt** of temper, they'll **blurt** out something **curt**. They might even say you're a little **squirt**, and reason it's your just **desert**.

Then, come the following week, they're likely do it again, this time to a **Kurt**, a Harry, or a **Burt**.

Story 145

Around The Earth

Ships travel the **earth**, en-cir-cling its fat **girth**. They travel through channel and **firth**, from London to **Perth**, and home again from **berth** to **berth**.

They carry those goods of which another nation has a **dearth**. This brings both countries great **mirth**, for each enjoys a much greater **worth**.

Story 146

Elmhurst

In **Elmhurst**--beginning June **first**, lasting exactly one year to May **thirty-first**--there was a drought, history's **worst**. Ten thousand persons died of **thirst**.

What is **worse**--when the clouds finally **burst**, mud slid and twenty thousand more died **submersed**. Can you imagine a land more **accursed**!

Story 147

He Didn't Unnerve

Baseball fans love Reggie because he had power in **reserve** and he had spirit or **verve** (a fact easy to **observe**).

Most batters when struck by a ball will **unnerve**. Not Reggie! He had the **nerve** to remain in the batter's box to homer any **curve** a pitcher would **serve**. And this is why he did **deserve** ten times that of the highest-paid **reserve**.

Ĭ

Story 148

Women's Lib

As children, brothers and sisters are equally called **sibs**. However, as adults, some men, now and then, treat women as though they're still babies wearing **bibs**, playing in **cribs**.

So today women **squib** for **Women's Lib**, wanting much more than **Adam's Rib**.

☞ See *Story 189*

Story 149

Not Slick

Dick is a crazy **mick**
And **Rick** is a coun-try **hick**
Dick calls a rooster a **chick**
And **Rick** calls a river a **crick**
Dick has a pet **tick**
And **Rick** has a pet **brick**
Neither of them is men-tal-ly **quick**,
But neither of them cares a **lick**.

Story 150

"Diction" Practice

Drugs **addict**
Diseases **afflict**
Juries **convict**
Pictures **depict**
Weapons **inflict**
Fortune tellers **predict**
Pythons **constrict**
Landlords **evict**
Bombs **interdict**
Enemies **conflict**
Lies **contradict**
And parents **restrict**

Story 151

A Peculiar Kid

Sid was a pe-cu-liar **kid**. Although toothless, he chewed a tobacco **quid**. Although generally skinny, he had a fat **mid**.

He often **hid** from school to go to the track to wa-ger a "small **bid**." Consequently his grades **slid**, as he took a fi-nan-cial **skid**.

Yes! This is what the silly six-year old **did**.

☞ See *Story 191*

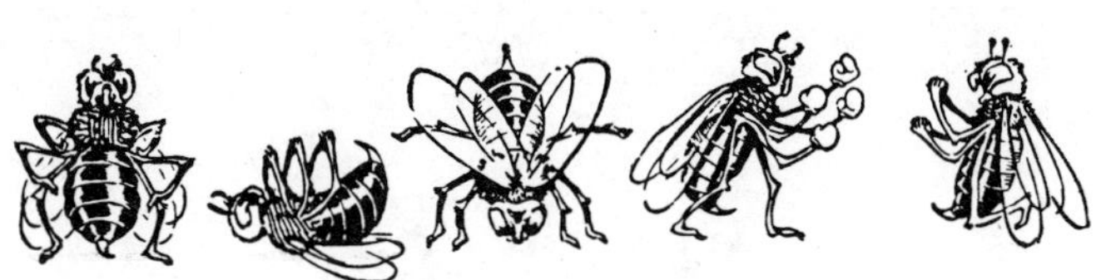

Story 152

The Bothersome Midge

Bob, Ted, Carol, and Sue--hiking on a mountain **ridge**--stopped at a spot overlooking a **bridge**.

They had planned to eat **spinach**, **porridge**, and **cabbage**; then to play **cribbage** and **bridge**. But before they could eat a **smidge**, they were chased off by a pestering, biting **midge**.

Story 153

Poor Biff

At the start of their camping **trip** Sue and **Biff** got into a **tiff**. She blamed everything on "blameless" **Biff**.

She complained of a skunk **whiff**, the cold air that made her nose **sniff**, and their climb up a **cliff** that made her back **stiff**.

So for the rest of their trip **Biff** had to bear her peevish **miff**.

☞ See *Story 193*

Story 154

A Lovers' Rift

Every now and again every married couple will have a **rift** and apart **drift**.

Then it becomes time for him to forget **thrift** and buy her a nice **gift**. Perhaps she'd like a slip or a **shift**. Either **gift** should give their re-la-tion-ship a **swift** and hefty **lift**.

Story 155

Gigged

So prim and proper was **Miss Kreig** that some said she was a stuffy **prig**. But then there came a Russian **shindig** whereat she drank vodka **swig** after **swig**. And on her knees she danced a **jig**, stuffing her face with dates and a **fig**.

As if this weren't enough, she called the Czar a "Fascist **pig**," struck him with an olive **twig**, then dared pull off the Czarina's horsehair **wig**.

For this **Miss Kreig** was given "life" in a Russian **brig**.

Story 156

Jack and Jill

Jack and **Jill** went up the **hill**, not to fetch a pail of water, but to fish for **brill** in a **swilling rill**.

However, they caught nothing or **nil**.

And when they came down, they came down with a **chill** and began to feel **ill**. So then their mother served them soup with **dill** and gave them each a get-well **pill**.

Story 157

Zilch

When the farmer is away
The cat will play
And **filch**[1] milk
From the farmer's **milch** cow
Leaving **zilch**
For baby in **pilch**[2] and Momma Sow

1) To steal.

2) An infant's protective garment worn over a diaper.

Story 158

Gilded

The church **guild** has **willed** not to **rebuild**, but to have the church's cracks **filled**, and to give the statues a lustrous **gild**.

This will make the bishop **thrill**, for his **till will** remain **filled** to the **gill**!

Story 159

The Crooked Ilk

Gangsters, robbers, and others of this **ilk** are the ones who dream up the schemes in which to **bilk**; such as adding water to **milk** or selling cheap cloth that will pass as **silk**.

Story 160

The House That Jack Built

For two whole years Jack worked, singing songs in the gayest **lilt**.

But after his house was finally **built**, he discovered that he couldn't walk within . . . without things being **spilt**. Before long he realized that his house was sitting on a **tilt--tilting**, **tilting**, **tilting**, more and more. Soon one **stilt** began to sink deep into the soft **silt**.

Unfortunately poor Jack was already in debt to the **hilt**, and therefore unable to have his house **rebuilt**.

What's more, his girl Jill gave him the **jilt**.

Story 161

Reason Or Whim?

Tim asked **Jim** to play with **him** and **Kim**. "No," replied **Jim**, "I can't go to the **gym**, I must fix my tire **rim**. But maybe later we can go for a **swim**?"

"But later," said **Tim**, "the sun will be too **dim**. Besides, your task is so hard and **grim** that you'll lose your vigor and **vim**."

Jim responded, "I don't know if this be reason or **whim**, but indeed I do want to stay **slim** and **trim**. So I'll put off fixing my bike **rim** and hurry off with you and **Kim**."

☞ See *Story 197*

Story 162

The Imp

Bobby is a brazen **imp**. He calls his brother a "**fat blimp**," and tells his sister her hair is always so **limp** that she shouldn't bother to **primp**?" Once he even demanded of his mother never to **scrimp** on groceries like **shrimp**.

So now and again his father, or mother would say, "Oh, **Imp**! . . . In your style I must put a **crimp**. And with my paddle I promise not to **skimp**!"

Story 163

"Captain Quinn"

"Capt." Quinn, who lives in a trash **bin**, says, "I love my cozy **inn**. It's a great place to collect bottles and **tin**, to fall asleep listening to traffic **din**, and to have bugs crawl all over my **skin**--from my **shin** to my **chin**. And eating just rats keeps me **thin**.

"Because I've given away my wealth to my kith and **kin**, now and then I must bum a **fin** to buy some **gin**.

"However, this be no **sin** and puts on my face a great big **grin**." ☞ See *Story 198*

Story 164

Quince

When a **blintz** was served to **Prince Vince** he shouted, "Nay, bring me pie and make it ***mince*** *without the meat*!"

The chef ad-mit-ted he never heard of ***mince*** *without the meat*, so he served him an ex-o-tic pie called **quince**. But one bite made the **prince wince**. "Water," he yelled, "my mouth needs a **rinse**!"

Con-se-quent-ly, **quince** has never **since** been served to the fin-ick-y **prince**.

Story 165

It Wasn't A Cinch

The fans thought the game would be a **cinch**.

But time was now running out and they began to yell, "**Lynch** the QB . . . **Lynch** the QB . . . **Lynch** the QB . . . ." This made the quarterback **flinch**. What a **pinch** he was in!

In desperation he winged a pass that flew like a **finch**[1], that was caught inbounds by scarcely an **inch**. Thus victory and the championship their team would **clinch**.

1) A bird.

Story 166

On A Binge

When the drunkard finally came home from a drunken **binge**, he ripped the front door right off its **hinge**. Then he tripped on the rug's **fringe** and hit his head and began to **twinge**.

Upon his face came a ghostly **tinge**, and upon his wife's face came a dis-gust-ing **cringe**.

☞ See *Story 181*

Story 167

Her Hospital Stint

As the runners started their **sprint**, Rawanda slipped and fell. Her broken leg had to be set in a **splint**.

Friends brought her candy, flowers, and **mint**. And there in the hospital, during her month-long re-cov-er-y **stint**, by **dint** of hard work, she learned how to perfectly **print**.

Story 168

On An Ocean Trip

On a fun **trip**, they **zipped** along at a fast **clip**, while porpoises below would do ac-ro-ba-tic **flips**.

Their **ship** had a pool in which swimmers would take an oc-ca-sion-al **dip**; but mostly the passengers would sit around eating potato **chips** with various **dips**.

Aboard **ship** was a pe-cu-liar man named **Skip**, who made everyone laugh with one after another **quip**. Evidently, though, he had lost his **grip**: he wore a woman's see-through **slip**, and he lit cigars with ten-dollar **scrip**. What's more, he called his liquor bill a **gyp**, then refused to give his waiter a proper **tip**.

☞ See *Story 200*

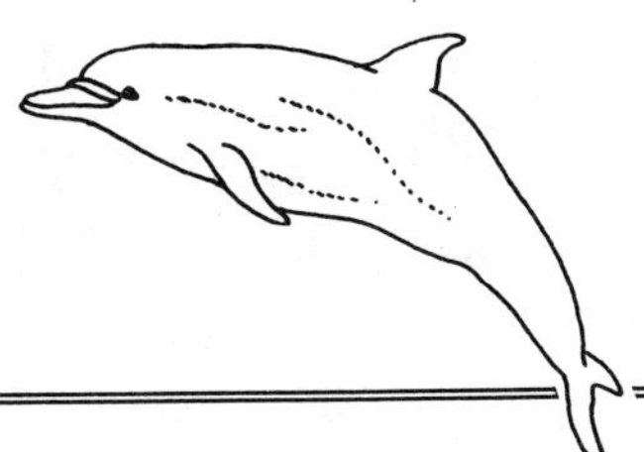

Story 169

No Script!

The actress **quipped**
I will be laid in a tomb or **crypt**
As dead as the pharaohs of **Egypt**
Before I read lines of any **script**.
My fans shall not be **gypped**
My style has never been **clipped**
So now, as before, my public will hear
Only ad-libbed words that I have **lipped**

Story 170

The Swiss Miss

Oh the land of **Swiss** is a land of **bliss**. You ask, why is **this**? It's because every **miss** always looks so prim and **priss**.

And although little boys may **hiss**, none can **resist** the maiden's sweet, sweet **kiss**.

Story 171

A Tasty Dish

Oh how I **wish**
That I could catch the **fish**
That makes the water **swish**
For it would make such a tasty, tasty **dish**

Story 172

Frisked

Seeing him take a golden **disk**, the policeman had to **frisk Mr. Brisque**. Isn't thievery always a big **risk**? Now off to jail he'll go **briskly whisked**, where he will eat nothing but bread and **bisque**.

Story 173

Holy Chrism

God's light shines on us as sunlight through a **prism**. It blesses us like Holy **Chrism** and keeps His Church from having another **schism**. It also reminds us of that dreadful di-lu-vi-al **cat-a-clysm** men-tioned in the Bible as well as the *Baltimore* ***Cat-e-chism***.

Story 174

Don't Lisp These "Isps"

There is

The smoke **wisp**
The brush **wisp**
The lettuce **crisp**
The breeze **crisp**
The picture **crisp**
The toast **crisp**
The noise **crisp**
The air **crisp**
The answer **crisp**
The speech **lisp**
And the leaves **lisp**

Story 175

A Lovers' Tryst

Dad gave to **Sis** a long **list** stating why he must **insist** that her love affair should not **exist**.

Still **Sis** tried to **twist** father's **wrist**, but every time father would **resist**, often even pounding his **fist**.

Yet the lovers would not **de-sist**, and began secretly to **tryst**.

Story 176

Pig On A Spit

About midnight the pig was **fit** on the **spit** and placed over the charcoal **pit**. So that **it** wouldn't burn, a close watch had to be kept on **it**.

At noon the next day girls came, some wearing sweaters--mostly **knits**--and dresses with **slits**. They were es-cort-ed by boys who brought bats, balls, and **mitts** to shag flies and take **hits**.

At two o'clock watermelons were **split** and seeds **spit**. Next the pig was removed from the **pit,** then eaten for hours to the last **bit** just as the sun was about to **quit**.

☞ See *Story 202*

3 Very Special Guests

Story 177

The Fritches

Mr. Fritch said to his son, "Ap-par-ent-ly, **Mich**, you don't care a **stitch** about finding your **niche** and becoming even moderately **rich**. Your be-hav-ior is giving me a anxious **twitch**.

"To get you a job, many times I have given a boss a sales **pitch**. But as fast as you're hired, you're fired. You get the **itch**. 'The job has a **hitch**,' you say. Then to another job you **switch**.

"Speaking of **switch**, when you were younger you should have gotten my **switch**. Then today maybe you wouldn't be in such a **ditch**.

"You ought to go back to school, **Mich**, and begin by learning to spell tricky words like the pronoun **which**, a **sandwich**, and the **Wicked Old Witch**."

Story 178

A Myth

Across the Atlantic's **width**
Along a Norwegian **frith**
Among his kin 'n' **kith**
There lives a man, **Goldsmith**
Who shoes unicorns as a **blacksmith**

Nowadays I buy my horseshoes
from Thom McAn!
He's one heck of a man!

Story 179

Kicks At Six

If a parent were to **mix** little boys with little girls--especially about the age of **six**--and leave them alone, the children would certainly have **kicks**. But oh, what a **fix**!

Next time this parent would more than likely say "**nix**" to having such **kicks**!

Story 180

Liz Is A Dizz

Liz loves to see cola **fizz**
She loves to hear bacon **sizz**
And she loves to have her hair **frizz**
But she hates so much as a little **quiz**
WHY?
Because **Liz** is a **dizz**
And cer-tain-ly no **whiz**

ŋ

Story 181

Bells Shall Ring

Like a bee **sting**
The Princess has stung the **King**
His Majesty's head has gone **zing**, **zing**, **zing**
Song birds, **winging** about, have begun to **sing**
Love, as flowers, blossoms this **spring**!

The **King** has promised her
    A diamond **ring**
    A new castle **wing**
    And a garden with **swing**

In return, he has asked but for one **thing**:
"To the altar love is all you need **bring**.
But, my love, your love is nearly **everything**."

☞ See *Story 166*

Story 182

The Missing Link

When Rocksanne tried to swim,
    lead boots made her **sink.**
When she tried to **wink,**
    she could only **blink.**
When she tried to **think,**
    her brain was on the **blink.**
She couldn't even tell red from **pink.**
The poor girl was even troubled learning to **drink.**

Story 183

The "Inct" Precinct

A dinosaur is **ex-tinct**
An animal thought is **in-stinct**
A brief, to-the-point word is **suc-cinct**
A sharp color is **dis-tinct**
A blurry color is **in-dis-tinct**
And a chain is simply **linked**

Story 184

Mr. and Mrs. Finks

To cel-e-brate their mar-ri-age, he bought her, his new bride, a stole made of **minks** and a coat of **lynx**.

Then after dinner and **drinks**, he said, "My Dear **Mrs. Finks**, **methinks** 'tis now time for **forty winks**!"

Ī

Story 185

Don't Cry

As each day goes **by** and **by**, we should **try** not to **cry** even when our best plans go **awry**.

When the rain falls from the **sky**, it shouldn't bring tears to our **eye**. Nay, let a smile be our **reply**. Without rain, flowers would not grow so **high**, ducks would not be so **spry**, and little pigs would have no mud in their **sty**.

Remember that somewhere in the darkest **sky** God is forever **nigh**, loving us--even though we often wonder **why**.

Story 186

"Aye, Aye"

"**Good-bye**," said **Mrs. Bligh**, "**I** am going to **buy** some hair **dye**, a loaf of **rye**, and chicken to **fry**."

Mr. Bligh barked, "You'd best keep the bill from getting **sky high**!"

"**Aye, aye**! **I** certainly shall **try**!" **replied Mrs. Bligh** as she batted one **sly eye**.

Story 187

Climbing High

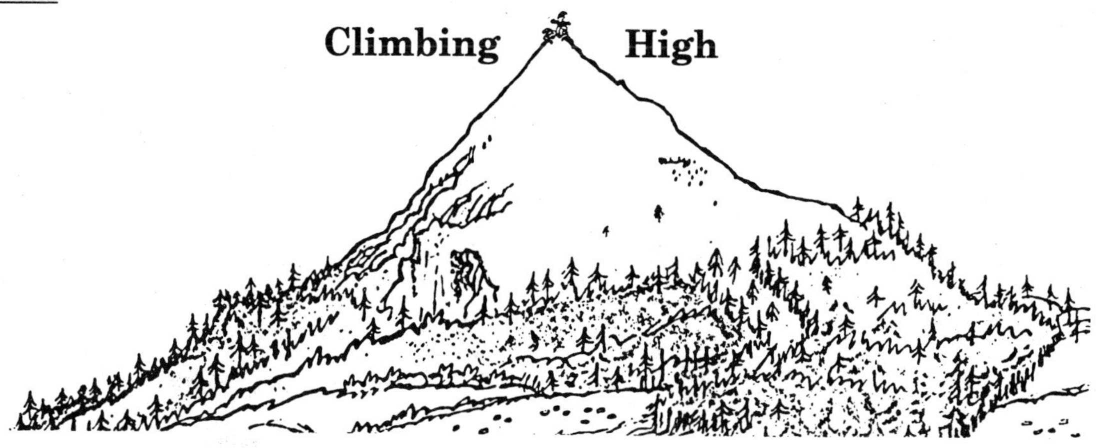

As the mountain top drew **nigh**, **Sy sighed** , "**I** thought we'd never climb so **high**! It is as though we're in the **sky**!"

"Yes," **replied Lu Lai**, "being on this mountain is a 'real **high**.' But, oh **my**! **By** tomorrow you and **I** shall pain from our toes to our **thigh**."

Story 188

A Pie-Eating Contest

How Jim and **Guy** did **vie** to eat the most apple **pie**! They ate as though it were do or **die**, for neither wanted to lose or **tie**.

Regardless of how hard Jim did **try**, he couldn't top the *ninety-nine* pieces eaten by **Guy**.

Now, had **I** not seen this with my very own **eye**, **I'd** say that this was one a-tro-cious **lie**!

Story 189

Bribed

The **scribe** reports that the pitcher has "thrown" the game for the **Tribe**.

He says, "**Ed Kyb** grew tired of the fans **jibe**, and took a **bribe**. He got $5,000 and a free paint job from **Earl Schieb**."

See *Story 148*

Story 190

A Thinking Device

Did you know that smoking is an unhealthy **vice**,
And that smoking in public is not very **nice**?
Did you know that things done fast are done in a **trice**?
Did you know that a louse and a louse make two **lice**?
Did you know that **thrice** is just one more than **twice**?
Did you know that one die plus another die make a pair of **dice**,
Did you know that Ginger and Rosemary are sisters and **spice**?
And did you know that hot dogs sell at a "beefed-up" **price**?

See *Story 206*

Story 191

The Young Bride

To **bide** her time a young **bride** may do things alone **outside**. She may take a car **ride** to the **seaside** where she may stroll with a lei-sure-ly **stride**, wade in the ocean **tide**, and simply watch sea gulls **glide** by.

But when she becomes a mother, baby shall be by her **side**, and she shall be his trusting **guide**. Now and then she may take him on a pony **ride**, or perhaps down a water **slide**. And almost always she'll beam with overflowing **pride**.

See *Story 151*

Story 192

Cry It!

For a few cents, you can **buy it**.

With a little butter, you can **fry it**.

Without butter, you can **try it** on a **diet**.

At Easter, you can also **dye it**.

And in **disquiet**, you can **fly it** to partake in a **riot**.

. . . Well, what is it, **Wyatt**?

Story 193

Strife Is Rife!

Ed said, "**Wife**,
I thought that our **life**
would
be
music
from
a
fife!

But our **life**
has been **rife**
with **strife**

So, dear **wife**,
please
lend
me
your
knife!

For I'm about to take your **life**!"

See Story 153

Story 194

Alike

Mike and **Ike** are so **alike**. They both **like** to whistle **like** the **wood shrike**. They both **like** to pedal a **unibike**. Both **like** to mountain **hike**. And both **like** to fish for **pike**, 'though neither has ever had a **strike**.

Story 195

A Lady of Inimitable Style

There once lived a lady of in-im-i-ta-ble **style**. Her abode was on a small Med-i-ter-ra-ne-an **isle**, about a **mile** from the mouth of the river **Nile**.

Her house was built of marble **tile**. And everything in it was in im-pec-ca-ble **file**.

Her behavior was never **vile**. And even though every man weakened at her **smile**, none was able to pass her **trial** and walk her down the wedding **aisle**.

Story 196

A Precious Child

"**Kyle** is a precious **child**. He never gets **riled**," his mother said as she **smiled**. "Watching TV often makes children **wild**, but watching none has made him **mild** and gentle **styled**."

Story 197

A Nursery Rhyme

You should know:

A lemon's shaped like a **lime**
Two nickels equal one **dime**
The choicest meat is **prime**
And gangsters cause **crime**

Also you should know:

Grease 'n' **grime**
Are a lot like **slime**
Mim-ic-ry is a lot like **mime**
Clamber is a lot like **climb**

And **cyme** grows somewhat as does **thyme**
But **thyme** is nothing like **time**
For **time**--listen to church bells **chime**.

☞ See *Story 161*

Story 198

At Nine

When I was **nine**, living on the river **Rhine**, the whole world was **mine**. In the morn I'd arise feeling **fine**, us-u-al-ly to **sun-shine** filtering through poplar and **pine**. Then outside I'd go to pick grapes from the **vine**, for which Dad always gave me a sip of **wine**.

Often I'd grab my fishing **line** or simply a ball of **twine** and, with my sister, Sweet **Ad-e-line**, fish the salty **brine**.

Now fish was **fine**, but we preferred to **dine** on **swine**, **bo-vine**, or **por-cu-pine**. In any case, Dad always drank his **moon-shine** in his **Al-pine stein**.

☞ See *Story 163*

Story 199

Develop Your Mind

Jahrell and Jerome are two of a **kind**. Neither pays his teacher any **mind**. They say that school's a **grind**, and that homework is so **unkind**. Con-se-quent-ly, they are both far **behind**.

Someday, however, they won't be so **blind**. They shall un-doubt-ed-ly **find** that the world's **unkind** to the ig-no-rant **mind**.

Story 200

Blood of Every Type

All wars create a great deal of **hype**
Especially for boys not fully **ripe**
They are the boys forbidden to **gripe**
They are the boys guer-ril-las will **snipe**
Will mothers ever have fewer tears to **wipe**?

☞ See *Story 168*

Story 201

The Brave Squire

In Great Britain, in a town **shire**, in a great mansion with a huge **spire**, works a **squire** for a lady much **higher**.

He always dresses in be-fit-ting **attire** and works without **tire** though he doesn't **perspire** even when mending miles of fence **wire**.

He has forded his lady across muddy **mire** and he has saved her prized **sire** from a barn **fire**.

Now he's her heart's **desire**, while she's his passion **fire**. Soon he shall **aspire** to the rank **esquire**, then marry and likely **retire**.

☞ See *Stories 132, 351*

Story 202

The Writer's Plight

A journalist **might write** to **incite** the lib-er-al left or the con-ser-va-tive **right**, thus start a little **fight**. Or she **might write** simply to provide the reader with **insight**.

At times, however, it's a **mite** dif-fi-cult to **write** when there is nothing im-por-tant to **cite**. Yet it's the **writer's** duty to **write** even with trivia so **trite**. Whatever the case, the paper is always **right** for making an excellent **kite**!

☞ *See Story 176*

Story 203

The Flight of The Playwright

"'In days of old when **knights** were bold--' is corny and old," said the **knight** to the **playwright**. "And further, it's a **slight** to every gal-lant **knight**."

At once the **playwright** knew he was in a dan-ger-ous **plight**, and started to shake with **fright**. "There will be a **fight**," said the beswordeded **knight**. "In the **bright moonlight**, **tonight** at **midnight** will be just **right** for a bloody **sight**."

Now the **playwright**, who lacked **might**, had the **foresight** to know he couldn't win this **fight**. He also knew that the impending **fight** would **likely blight** his **height**.

So, **politely** he answered: "Sorry, dear **knight**, perhaps some other **night**. You see, **tonight** my plans are too very **tight**. So good **night**, you bad, brave **knight**." Then away he fled at the speed of **light**.

Story 204

Not Blithesome

The sharecropper works the fields with a **scythe**
The hard work keeps his body very **lithe**
Though of the profit he keeps but a **tithe**
Thus the songs that he sings are not so **blithe**
For deep inside his spirit does **writhe**

Story 205

How Success Arrives

It is not enough mere-ly to be **alive**. We must **strive** to op-ti-mal-ly **thrive**. We must have the **drive** to work past **five**, as busy bees in a **hive**. Then, and only then, shall success **arrive**.

Story 206

Unwise

It's **unwise** to **arise** much after **sunrise**
It's **unwise** to make **buys** of **Levis** of the wrong **size**
It's **unwise** to **devise lies** to win any **prize**
And it's **unwise** to harshly **criticize**,
Knowing that later you're likely to **apologize**

☞ See *Story 190*

AH or AW

AH or AW

Story 207

At The Spa

"**Pa**, how's about goin' to the **spa**?" asked **Ma** to her husband, **Mr. I. Saah**.

He answered, "**Bah**! Only girls use a **spa**! Why for do you think **spa** rhymes with **bra**?"

"**Ha**!" exclaimed **Mrs. C. Saah**. "I've seen **Mr. Hugh Baugh** using the **spa**, and I heard 'm comment, '**Ah**.'"

Story 208

They Began To Sob

Bob and **Rob** were called "**The Blob**" and "**The Squab**," respectively, and "**The Slobs**" collectively.

They thought about becoming Navy **gobs**, but refused, not liking their would-be **jobs** of mopping ship decks with **swabs**. So they started to **hobnob** with the **mob**. Soon they pulled their first bank **job**. Caught red handed, they immediately began to **sob**.
In jail they would con-tin-u-al-ly **sob**, realizing how stupid it was to **rob**.

☞ See *Story 248*

Story 209

Father Bach

While the **cock** crows, **Father Bach** dresses into his **frock** and puts on his holey **socks**. Then he eats breakfast of either bagels and **lox** or eggs and **hocks**.

Afterward he'll walk a **block** to the **dock** of the **loch** to fish the waters so **chock** full of **rock**.

Come afternoon he dresses into a **smock** to butcher one of the abbey's beef **stock** or a few of their feathery **flock**.

Then around six **o'clock**, he cooks supper in a **crock** as he drinks his beer called Ba-var-i-an **bock**.

Story 210

On Cape Cod

Ms. Todd, who lives on **Cape Cod**, fishes daily for **scrod**. On her **sod** she grows green peas and sells them in the **pod**.

Being ever so grateful for little things, every Sunday she'll **trod** to church, bow her head, and thank her **God**.

☞ See *Story 250*

Story 211

Rodge

Rodge ate so much fattening **stodge**
That he grew a huge **podge**
And couldn't get through the door of his **lodge**
Nor onto the front seat of his **Dodge**
So he took a job as a farm **hodge**
Hoping for his fat to **dislodge**

AH or AW

Story 212

Outside of Prague

Away from the **smog** of **Prague,** there lives a young man with his **dog** in a hut of cedar **log**.

To support himself he raises **hogs** and makes wooden shoes called **clogs**.

Early every morning he puts on his **togs** and **jogs** through the **smoggy, soggy bog.** Afterward he'll drink **eggnog** or a bottle of **grog** and serve his lucky **dog** scrump-tious legs of un-lucky **frog**.

Story 213

After The Prom

After the **prom**, brothers **Dom** and **Tom** said goodbye to their **Mom** and went to fight in **Viet Nam**. **Dom** fired mortars that went **pom**, **pom**, and **Tom** dropped the napalm **bomb**.

And after **Viet Nam**, **Dom** and **Tom** married sisters Susie and Sara **Wom**, whom they met on the island of **Guam**.

AH or AW

Story 214

Palm Sunday

On **Palm Sunday** the choir shall sing some **calm psalms** that will soothe souls like **balm**.

No soul shall express any **qualm**. All shall give **alms**, sing songs, and wave **palms**.

Story 215

Back to the Swamp

The Frog Prince said, "My pretty miss, how I shall miss your pag-eant-ry and **pomp**! But my Dear, I fear my met-a-mor-pho-sis is near. Big feet will soon loudly **clomp**, and likely upon me **stomp**. Therefore, off I must **romp** to the safety of some nearby **swamp**!"

Story 216

John

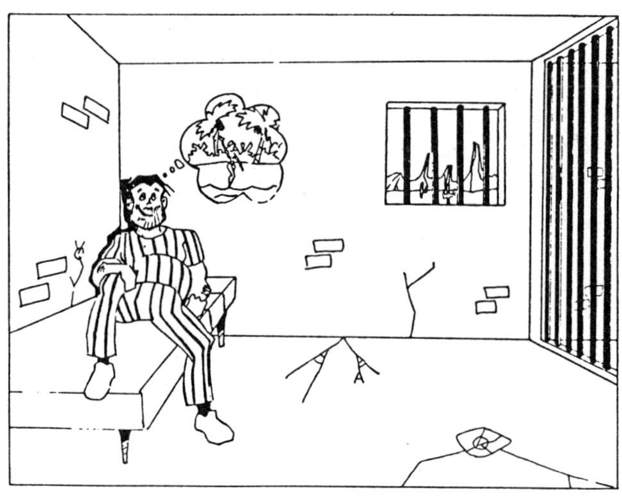

John was a **con** jailed in **Tucson** for stealing a goose and a long-necked **swan**. He was given striped clothes to **don,** or in other words to put **on**.

Although his hopes for parole were **wan**, still he dreamt of being far **gone** to a land far **yon** to start a new life with his waiting wife, **Yvonne**.

☞ See *Story 317*

Story 217

Pig Slop and Soda Pop

The thief stole a bottle of soda **pop** from **Dunlop's** barber **shop**.

Mr. Dunlop, having but one leg, had to **hop**. But he pursued, swinging his leather **strop**.

He chased the thief **plop** into a **cop** who gave his neck a ka-ra-te **chop**; his kisser, a **pop**; and his head, a **bop**. For minutes he spun 'round like a **top**. When finally he **stopped**, he **dropped** to the ground and **flopped**.

In jail he was fed nothing but pig **slop**, and, as a reminder, that very same brand of **pop**.

☞ See *Story 261*

AH or AW

Story 218

Josh

Josh hates to **wash**. But he loves to **swash** in rain-filled puddles, wearing neither rubbers nor **mack-in-tosh**.

When eating, he **sloshes** his jeans with **nosh** or **squash**, causing his mother to yell, "**Tosh** . . . **tosh**! By **gosh**, someday I hope to **quash** your be-hav-ior with a befitting **kibosh**!"

Nevertheless **Josh** merely shrugs his shoulders and says, "Oh, **posh**!"

Story 219

Overtaking The Penobscots

General Scott summoned every officer to **plot** a plan to capture the **Penobscots**. "Because our horses are too tired even to **trot**," he said, "we will sneak attack in **yachts**, slowly at five **knots**."

While the Indians were dining on beans, **kumquat**, and **whatnot**, **Scott** sailed out and overtook the **Penobscots**, firing **not** one single **shot**.

☞ See *Story 264*

Story 220

Scotch

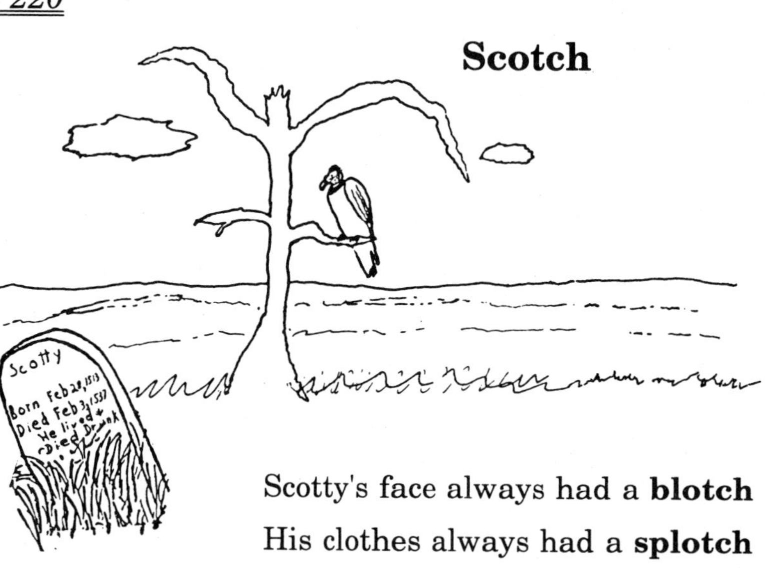

Scotty's face always had a **blotch**
His clothes always had a **splotch**
And every job he ever had he'd **botch**
Therefore he never moved up a **notch**
Why?
Johnnie Walker Scotch

AH or AW

Story 221

The Goths

Cen-tur-ies ago there lived a Ger-man-ic race called the **Vis-i-goths**, known also as the **Os-tro-goths**, or merely the **Goths**. The Romans said that the **Goths** were bar-bar-i-ans--lazy **sloths**.

This so angered the **Goths** that it filled their hearts with **wroth**. The **Goths** turned into "mad men" spewing **froth**. Soon one after another Roman fell by the **swaths** of the be-sword-ed **Goths**.

☞ See *Story 266*

Story 222

Albert Knox

Albert Knox catches salmon, called **lox**, and sells them frozen by the **box**. He grows cotton to make **socks**, and raises hogs especially for **hocks**.

To till his fields he uses a bull **ox**. He keeps a few **gamecocks** too, because they protect his chickens from **fox** and are more dependable than the best alarm **clocks**.

Story 223

Nearly Every "Azh"

The soldier's **cam•ou•flage**

The aerial **bar•rage**

The desert **mi•rage**

The twenty-four room **mé•nage**

The king's **en•tou•rage**

The two-car **garage**

The flower **cor•sage**

The body **mas•sage**

The enemy's **sab•o•tage**

The discussion's **per•si•flage**

And this word **collage**.

☞ See Stories *8*, *41*, *152*

AW

Story 224

The Crows That Can't Caw

Chief Big Paw makes tribal **law**, and his **squaw Long Claw** makes **coleslaw**. **Big Paw gnaws** bear meat **raw** with a one-toothed **jaw**, and **Long Claw draws** soda through a bamboo **straw**.

Although both are Crow, neither can **caw**. But their bird, a **macaw**, can **caw**.

Summer through fall they hunt along the **Arkansas**, from the river to **Omaha**. In winter they mostly **draw** and play on a **seesaw**. Come spring, when the river begins to **thaw**, they'll hem and **haw** and **hee haw**, then dive into the cold **Arkansas** and swim in the **raw**.

Story 225

Thanks to Maude

Maude knew at once that the "diamonds" were **fraud**--actually worthless **gaud**.

Why did **Maude** suspect **fraud**? Because of the nervous way the salesman hemmed and **hawed**, and his slip of the tongue--he called her a "**broad**."

So thanks to **Maude**, whom we **laud**, the police were able to arrest this **fraud**.

AH or AW

Story 226

Don't Scoff

At the mention of work, the lazy boy **oft** would **scoff**, unless the work were very **soft**.

Well, one day he started to **hiccough**. So he went to the water "**trough**" and began to **quaff**. His boss, *ticked **off***, thinking that he was likely *goofing **off***, said, "That's once too **oft**!" And dis-charged him *right **off***.

Story 227

In The Loft

On a choice **toft**, on a small **croft**, there lived an Englishman who **oft** slept **aloft** in a **hayloft**.

He preferred the **loft** despite how he **coughed**, which had his wife think his head was **soft**. But in truth, had she known of the liquor he **quaffed**--she would have much, much more than **scoffed**.

Story 228

He Started A Brawl

Billy Joe, slurring in a Texas **drawl**, was so in-e-bri-a-ted that his hand writing looked like **scrawl**.

When he fell off his barstool, he could barely **crawl**, yet he managed to snatch a lady's **shawl**, thus starting a **brawl**.

This caused his poor wife to break down and **bawl**.

Story 229

The Fall Ball

Saul, my old friend, gave me a **call**. He said, "Please go to the **Fall Ball** with my friend **Paul**. He is quite handsome and very **tall**."

But as it turned out, **Paul** was quite ugly and very **small**. I said to myself, "What **gall**!" So when **Saul** arrived at the dance **hall**, I slapped him against the **wall**, then yanked him outside onto the grassy **mall**, where I clobbered him silly with a wooden **maul**.

Story 230

In Times Of Auld

In times of **auld**[1], now and then when the Crown **called**, young knights often **squalled**, some even **bawled**.

In battle they feared being **mauled**--or worse, having their heads **fall** and scalped **bald**.

Nonetheless, "Cry Babies" was still what they were **called**.

1) Olden times.

Story 231

A Balk

If a pitcher were to commit a **balk** and then, at the ump, in mock dis-be-lief **gawk** and **back talk**, the fans might say--"What a **squawk**!" The ump might say, "Take a **walk**!"

Then, e-jec-ted, off the mound the pitcher would **stalk**.

AH or AW

Story 232

Whose Fault?

It's not my **fault**, said fat boy **Walt**
That I can neither jump nor **vault**,
For I am unable to **halt**
My craving for spices like **salt**,
And sugar, especially in **malt**.

Story 233

The Schmaltzy Waltz

Debra Walts said to herself, "I enjoy music that's lively, not **schmaltz**! So why did I dance all night to **schmaltz** like the Tennes-see **Waltz**?

"Now my feet must be soaked in **Epsom salts**."

Story 234

The Crime Was Solved

The crime was **solved**
An ac-com-plice was **involved**
The verdict **evolved**
Thus--
With the offenders' fate **resolved**,
The prison gates **re-volved**
As the men's good names **dis-solved**.

Story 235

Sean

Sean cashed in all he had to **pawn**
To move to the woods where he was **drawn**
To fish for trout upstream to **spawn**
To use an ax to build his **brawn**
To sleep upon grassy **lawn**
And wake at **dawn** with robust **yawn**,
Seeing bucks, does, and little **fawn**

Story 236

The Boat Launch

The fat boy said, "Kind friend--so dear, so **staunch**--please, oh please help me to **launch** my **launch**. I'd do it myself but for my big **paunch** and my big, big **haunch**."

The other replied, "Fat friend, if ever you're to lose your fat **paunch** and even fatter **haunch**, laziness is a habit you ought to **staunch**."

Story 237

His Last Jaunt

To save our souls was Jesus's **want**. So for forty days He fasted and grew deep-eyed and **gaunt**. He knew soon he would take His Calvary **jaunt**, and hear these jeers and **taunts**--

Vaunt your greatness!
Flaunt your crown of thorns!

Through it all his courage didn't **daunt**, though tearful were Mary and His **aunt**.

Story 238

The Blond

The pretty **blond** decided to break her city **bond** and move to the country far **beyond**.

There she would swim in clear-blue **pond** and **respond** to nature of which she was so **fond**.

Story 239

Right Is Wrong

Su Wong, a **Viet Cong**, walked a trail many miles **long**. When it forked Su didn't know which **prong** was right and which were **wrong**.

Just then she heard the **strong gong** of a church bell "**dong**." Then she knew to take the left **prong**. Soon she was one of the **throng**, walking **along** singing a hymnal **song**.

Story 240

Verbal Honky-Tonk

The geese **honked** out
Big Foot **clonked** out
Then the auto **conked** out
Then the sleepyhead **conked** out, too
And then last the snail **conked**[1] out, three

1) Conk: A sea shell.

Story 241

Haus

After **Haus** welded the railing and scraped away the **dross**, he shined it to a sparkling **gloss**. Yet his **boss** was **cross**. He yelled, "Shoddy workmanship will have me take a **loss**!" Then he came at **Haus**.

But **Haus** flew off like an **al-ba-tross**, swinging to safety on a live oak's **flossy** Spanish **moss**.

Story 242

Embossed

On a street that she **crossed**
Jennel slipped on some **frost**
Then again on a step **mossed**
Her dignity was **lost**
What's worse, now she bears a head **embossed**

Story 243

Fraught With Trickiness

The teacher said "Class, I'm ready to teach if you're ready to be **taught**.

"We **ought** to start with **ought**, usually spelled **ought** but sometimes **aught**. Likewise, **nought**--meaning nothing--may be spelled **nought** or **naught**.

"Never say catched for **caught**. Never say buyed for **bought**, nor brung for **brought**, nor fighted for **fought**. However, you may say either worked or **wrought**.

"Now, class, is it thinked or **thought**? Is goodness seeked or **sought**? And with a 'gh,' is a rope held **tau(gh)t**?"

Story 244

Santa Claus

There's always **applause**
For **Santa Claus**
Because
Of his **cause**
To give gifts to the **McGraws**
And to others who keep their momma's **laws**

Ō

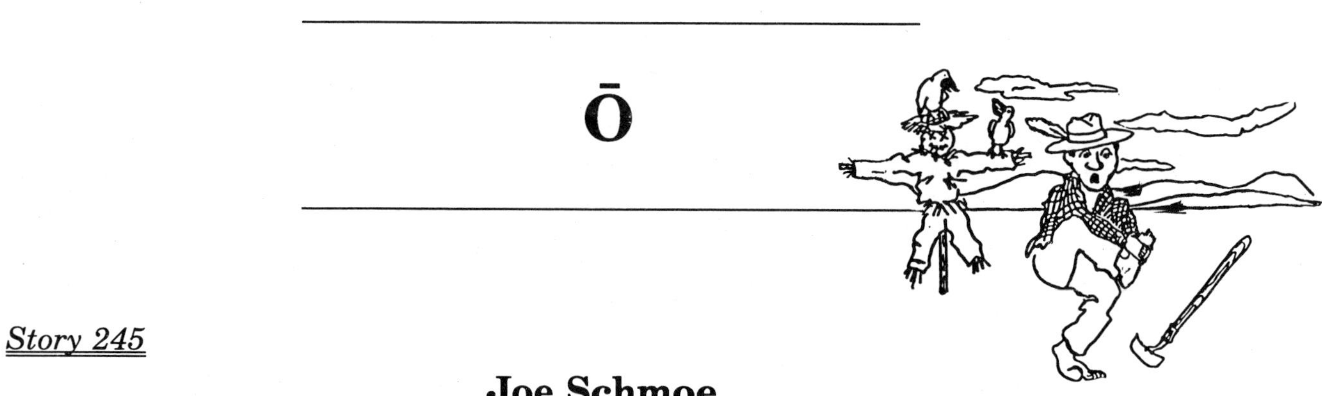

Story 245

Joe Schmoe

Joe Schmoe used to **go** a fishing for shad **roe**. That is, until he was struck by an ice **floe**, then he opted for hunting **roe**--both hind and **doe**. Soon, **though**, he got shot smack in the **elbow** with an **arrow**.

After this he gave hunting a rest to stick to that which he knew best: **mow** grass, **hoe** soil, **sow** seeds, and **grow** plants--such as **to-bac-co**, **to-ma-to**, and **po-ta-to**. But again he was beset by **woe**: this time a common **crow** pecked off his big **toe**.

Story 246

Margot and Her Beau

Margot com-plain-ed to her **beau**, "Do you ever plan to marry me, **Moe**?"

He answered, "**Although** I love you **so**, **Margot**, there are many debts that I still **owe**. I simply cannot af-ford a bottle of **Bordeaux**, let along a **bun-ga-low**. However, if I should stumble across some **dough**, then off to the marriage rail we shall **go**!"

"**Oh**!" exclaimed **Margot**, "Is that **so**! **Ergo--heigh-ho**! It's high time you get your hat and **go**!"

Story 247

The Show Below

Margeaux and **Flo** loved to **go** to a certain spot on a hilltop, which was ad-jacent to a **bow** of a river **below**.

Up there they could always feel a gentle wind **blow**, and see the sun glisten and **glow** on the **slow** river **flow** and on the fields whenever there was **snow**. There they could hear the **crow** caw and the rooster **crow**.

There they came to **know** how farmers **mow** weeds, **sow** seeds, **grow** peas, and **stow** in their **silos** whatever crops they please. Moreover, they found out what farming is all about--not an easy **show**, but a very hard **row** to **hoe**.

☞ See *Story 271*

Story 248

Mrs. Loeb

On a trip around the **globe** an earring came off her **earlobe**.

So **Mrs. Loeb** called on the police of the city of Nice, in-sis-ting that they **probe**. But by **Job**! all along that earring had been right in the left pocket of her **robe**.

☞ See *Story 208*

Story 249

No Poaching

As night was about to **approach,** Tikeisha began to fish for **loach**. At first she tried bait, a live **roach**, which she carried in her **brooch**. Having no luck, she pulled out a light and began to **poach**.

However, *she* soon was caught and then given a very stiff **re-proach**.

Story 250

An Ode To a Toad

Wharton was an in-spi-ra-tion to every **toad** whose **abode** was a pond by the side of the **road**.

His splash **bode** happiness, and it clearly **showed**, for the frogs faces brightly **glowed**. It was kindness that he **sowed**.

His personal **code** made him carry more than just his **load**, for from his heart love **flowed**. In troubled waters he often **rowed** his lily frond through the breakers of their pond to rescue many a **discom-moded toad**.

☞ See *Story 210*

Story 251

The Rogue

Un-friend-ly as an elephant **rogue**, the loner refuses to wear any clothes in **vogue**. He cares not to talk or **collogue**, and when he does it's in a pe-cu-liar **brogue**.

He only likes to be alone to fish for **togue** upon a pond in a **pirogue**[1]

1) A small boat.

Story 252

The Lazy Bloke

The lazy **bloke** before noon never **awoke**. The rest of the day he drank case after case of **coke** and blew rings of cig-a-rette **smoke**, so many so that one would nearly **choke**.

He said, "It isn't a **joke**! Work makes me want to **croak**, par-a-lyz-ing me as if by a **stroke**. Never, I say, will I be under another's **yoke**."

Thus, it's no surprise that this lazy **bloke** was nearly always **broke**.

Story 253

Under The Oak

When the rain fell not one of the **folk** had on a rain **cloak**. Yet nobody **croaked**, 'cause nobody got **soaked**.

They **stoked** up a fire under an **oak**, where they sat happily drink-ing their **coke** and munching egg **yolk** and hearts of **ar-ti-choke.**

Story 254

The Dead Sea Scrolls

On one morn about eleven
In the year '47
A Bedouin boy went out to **troll.**
When he heard the steeple bells **toll**
He docked his boat and took a **stroll**
That took him up upon a **knoll**
Where he found a cave with rare **bowls**
And the cen-tu-ries-old "**Dead Sea Scrolls**"
Which schol-ars were later to **unroll**
To find the Bible nearly in **whole**

Story 255

All But Charcoal

An-thra-cite and bi-tu-mi-nous
are two kinds of **coals.**

Large numbers and shal-low waters
are two kinds of **shoals.**

And staying clean and being good
are two kinds of . . . *impossible* **goals.**

Story 256

A Long Wait for Parole

When people are on the **dole**, it becomes hard for police to keep shop-lift-ing under **control**. Therefore, se-cur-i-ty guards must **patrol**, playing an im-por-tant **role** keeping coats and **stoles** secure on their **poles**.

None-the-less, many a sorry **soul** will steal such things as a silver **bowl** or even a **console**. And when caught, re-gard-less of what he **stole**, he likely will be given a prison **role**.

Story 257

Leopold

"Mother, please!" said **Leopold**. "I am too **old** for you to **scold**. If I have **told** you once, I have **told** you **twenty-fold**: I need to leave your **house-hold**. My reasons are **man-i-fold**. Living here makes me feel like a with-er-ing **marigold**.

"The journey I'll take is doubt-less-ly **bold**. I will travel through wood 'n' **wold** in my search for silver 'n' **gold**. But thoughts of you I shall always **behold**, and thus my heart shall never grow **cold**."

Story 258

The Animal Revolt

When the truck stopped a-brupt-ly with a **jolt**, it caused the cattle to snap the safety **bolt**.

As a **result**, all the animals began to **exult**, then quickly **bolt**. On the loose were ten squab-bling **poults** and as many **colts** and one goat who had not yet begun to **moult**.

It was an all-out animal **revolt**, that struck the trucker like a **thunderbolt**!

Story 259

Jerome

Jerome was born in **Nome.**'Til seven, 'twas Heaven,
But he left Alaska
For the state of Nebraska,
Then later on to **Rome**.
And this is where he is today
Living with his wife, sweet Kay.

Their house is a plush first-class **home**
With a blue tinted Plex-i-glas **dome**
In which they grow plants in **loam**

Their car is a spiffy Jaguar--
It's a coupe, with shining, sparkling **chrome**,
In which they like to **roam**
But their real joy is to read a **tome**
Con-tain-ing either novel or **poem**
Such as this silly one, "**Jerome**"

Story 260

Ruling The Throne

King Tyrone III so loved the smell of **cologne** that he asked **Princess Sharoan** to help him rule the **throne**. Happily they lived on the river **Rhone** in a castle built of **stone**.

All about the castle **zone** min-strels played the **trombone** and the **saxophone**. And on oc-ca-sion the king would **intone** a tune in **baritone**.

The King was **prone** to leave his guards **alone**; however, he did insist that they keep their muscles in **tone**, for which the **throne** gave them each a daily ice cream **cone**.

Story 261

He Prays For Moral Soap

The **Pope**, who is filled with **hope**, prays daily on his beaded **rope**. His prayers cover a large **scope**:

First and foremost he prays for the **mis-an-thrope**. He prays for boys and girls who can hardly **cope**, and for those who in darkness **grope**. He prays for the dis-o-be-di-ent who have chosen to **elope**, and for the self-pitying who do nothing but **mope**.

Last, but certainly not least, he prays for those hooked on **dope**, whose lives have taken a downward **slope**.

☞ See *Story 217*

Story 262

The Circus Is Grandiose

At the circus the ring leader is loud and **verbose**; the clown is jovial and **jocose**; the fat lady is **globose**, with rolls and rolls of **adipose**. And the freaks, they are **gross**. In another way, the elephants are **gross** too--and one whiff can be a potent **dose**!

Nevertheless, the show is always **grandiose**!

☞ See *Story 268*

Story 263

The Utmost Party

Once on Maine's **northern-most seacoast**, we were in-vit-ed by a **most** gra-cious **host** to a party that was truly the **utter-most**.

Modest **George Yost** would not in the least **boast**, but his yard would, with a lantern atop each **post**. We were served cav-i-ar on **toast** and the tastiest **roast**. Every guest proposed a **toast**, which was laughed down with a witty **riposte**.

The next day this **foremost** party was ballyhooed in *The New York Times* and ***The Washington Post***.

Story 264

A Slogan On Which To Dote

Can-di-date **Goldie Oats** mused, "I need a slogan that people will **note** . . . one on which they will **dote.** It must be something they can learn by **rote** and readily **quote**."

Sat-is-fied, she beamed and began to **gloat**. These two she would **emote**:

A **VOTE** FOR **OATS** WILL MAKE YOUR TAXES
EASY TO **TOTE**!

&

A *DARK HORSE*[1] NEEDS HER **VOTES**;
AS WE, THE PEOPLE, NEED OUR GOLDIE **OATS**!

1. A long shot or unlikely choice.

☞ See *Story 219*

Story 265

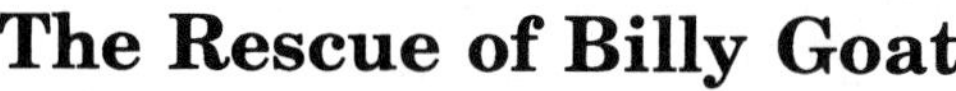

The Rescue of Billy Goat

Once while grazing on wild **oat,** Billy **goat,** wearing his real *100%* kid **coat**, tripped and fell into a castle **moat**. So much water swashed down his **throat** that he could barely stay **afloat**.

But lucky for the **goat**, the watchful Queen was taking **note** and rescued Billy in her **motorboat**.

Story 266

An Oath

They **both** took an **oath**. He promised never to act as a lazy **sloth**. She promised to keep her heart free from anger or **wroth**.

This was their **troth**, for they **both** wanted a boun-ti-ful marriage **growth**.

☞ See *Story 221*

Story 267

A Party Near The Cove

The host-ess put on her **mauve** sweater then **drove** to the market near the ocean **cove**, where she bought a ham and a garlic **clove**. Then she went to a certain **grove** having oranges that a-bun-dant-ly **throve**.

That evening guests came to her house in a **drove**. They tast-ed the ham prepared in her **stove** and exclaimed, "By **Jove**! How tasty garnished with oranges and **clove**! And how sin-gu-lar-ly perfect are these slices your cleaver **clove**!"

Story 268

Rose

In summer **Rose** often **arose** a couple hours after the sun **rose**. Near the day's **close** she would dress in gardening **clothes** to work her garden with a water **hose**, never with any raking **hoes**.

Then afterward she'd get herself into a comfortable **pose** to watch some TV **shows**. Soon again she'd find greater **repose** and begin to **doze**.

☞ See *Story 262*

Story 269

Had He Known

The cowboy should have **known** not to ride the **full-grown** bucking **roan**, because sky high he was **thrown**.

When he landed he let out a loud **groan**. For four hours he could do nothing but **moan**.

A whole week went by before his ill fate was finally **known**. Soon he'd join his dead wife **Joan**!

☞ See *Story 280*

Story 270

Jimmy Oaks

The "goody, goody" behavior of **Jimmy Oaks** is a sheer **hoax** to fool his teacher and his **folks**.

When they aren't around, he **smokes**! And once, with the help of a helper whom he had to **coax**, he stole a case of Pepsi and another of **Cokes**.

OU

Story 271

She Almost Broke Her Vow

Every day **Farmer Howe** milked ten head of **cow**, fed the piglets and a **sow**, tilled his fields with a **plough**, and stacked hay in a **mow**.

Hard work caused sweat to roll from his **brow**. He did everything he knew **how** to please his **frau**. But **Mrs. Howe** wouldn't even fix his **chow**. E-ven-tu-al-ly they got into a **row**. So she decided to take a **bow.**

However, swayed by a con-science that wouldn't **allow** a broken marriage **vow**, she soon returned crying, "I'll be better **now**, if only you'll show me **how**!"

☞ See *Story 247*

Story 272

Fond of Fowl

Once upon a time there lived a monk named **Father Powell**, who always wore a robe with a **cowl**.

At sin he would **scowl** and say, "It's **foul**!" But at food, he would **yowl**, especially for **fowl**.

Therefore he kept a bird dog that would **growl** and a coy-o-te that would **howl**. And at night, with the help of an **owl**, they would go out on the **prowl** to catch the tasty **water-fowl**.

Story 273

Mrs. Raoul

She fixes her chairs with a **dowel**
She finishes con-crete with a **trowel**
She goads her horse with a **rowel**
She dries herself off with a **towel**
And she greets people with a **bow**

Story 274

To Cal

My best **gal**
Sal
And I **shall**
F ly to **Cal**
To be with **Al**
And his **pal**
Hal
The **bac-cha-nal**
Time we **shall**
Have **shall**
Raise **mo-rale**

Story 275

The Grouch

Big sister can **vouch**
That mother's a **grouch**
She says, "Don't dare **slouch**"
And if we do dare--
From out her **pouch**
Her whip will make us say **OUCH**!

Story 276

Be Proud

Your honor should not have a **cloud**
When wrapped in a burial **shroud**
Now is the time to stand out from the **crowd**
Now is the time to make your parents **proud**
And now is the time to make angels sing **aloud**

Story 277

A Thorough Trouncing

On the rat the cat **pounced**
She shook the ro-dent with a **flounce**
Up . . . down--it did **bounce**
It was a tough and thorough **trounce**
Soon its strength ebbed to the last **ounce**
As "Chow" the cat was heard **announce**

Story 278

A Gold Pound

Walking with her **hound** on the beach of the **Sound,** a young girl **found** a gold **pound** in a sand **mound**.

She asked herself: "Was there a reef **around** on which a ship had run **a-ground**? To whom would this wealth **re-dound**? Would talking about it be **un-sound**?"

Her mind was **con-founded**, her con-science **hounded**. So deciding to make the state as **dumfounded** as she was **astounded**, she told how it lay **in-grounded**.

Story 279

Laziness Is Hard to Surmount

The **Count** cannot **count** to a very high **amount**. In fact, he cannot even **count** the few ducks in his **fount**. He cannot keep **ac-count** of the papers he stacks in a big **mount**. His horse he can't even **mount** or **dis-mount**. Things that happened as re-cent-ly as yesterday he often can't **re-count**.

Yet he defends himself saying, "Other things are more **par-a-mount**. And, besides, I have my trusty servants on whom to **count**, 1-2-3-4."

Story 280

Nouns, Etc.

An ad-jec-tive is a de-scrip-tive word like the color **brown**, or upside **down**.

A verb is an action word--as in the swimmer may **drown**, or the teacher may **frown**.

An adverb mod-i-fies a verb or another adverb: Rain is falling **down**; she is growing **round**.

A **pronoun** (such as who, where, which, what, this, that, these, those, his, hers, etc.) takes the place of a **noun**.

And a **noun** may be a person--a **clown**, a place--a **town**, or a thing like a king's **crown**, or an evening **gown**, or a goose's **down**.

☞ See *Story 269*

Story 281

How They Would Grouse!

When **Karl Kraus** told **Rebecca Grauss,** "Woman, why don't you change your ugly **blouse**?" she became in-fu-ri-ated and screamed at her would-be **spouse**.

"You're a little **mouse**, a lazy **louse**, and a drunken **souse**," she said. And then, with the point of her shoe, she kicked **Kraus** straight out of her **house**.

Story 282

Ousted

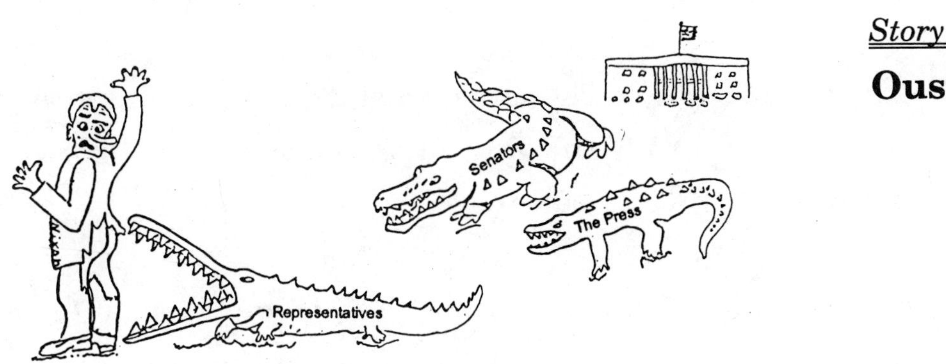

The "*left*" and the "*right*" began to **joust**. The "left" wanted Mr. Nixon **unhoused**. Then soon there came the Watergate **roust**, which proved to be the president's White House **oust**.

Story 283

Highly Touted

A hero they would **tout**
They used to yell 'n' **shout**
Why were they so **devout**?
What was it all **about**?
Here is the in and **out**--

The Boxer was big and **stout**
And had a lot of **clout**
Every **bout** was a **rout**
Won by **knockout**
By breaking either jaw or **snout**

Story 284

A Drought

It was the sad **truth** that it was drier than **vermouth**. It happened first in *Plymouth* and *Falmouth* and then in the **south** of the County **Louth**. There was a **drought**. Ten hundred folks died with a dried-up **mouth**.

Story 285

An Evil Power

The man was **dour**. The only normal thing he did was give the trees in his **bower** a daily **shower**. At passersby he would **glower** or **lower**, as they would **cower**.

At night he'd fry snakes in **flour**, then **devour** them at the midnight **hour**. Some people said they could sense the devil's **power**. ☞ See *Story 352*

Story 286

Impossible To Rouse

All night long some guys and **gals** like to **browse**, then in the morn they're impossible to **rouse**.

Not till noon do they put on a shirt or **blouse**, call their **pals**, or start to **unhouse**.

Idleness, they don't actually **espouse**, but instead of work, they would much rather **carouse**.

OR̃

Story 287

War In The Corps

When **Georgie Moore** turned **twenty-four** he had to go to **war**.

First he thought about the **Air Corps**, but he knew not how to **soar**. Next he thought about the Navy, but he knew not how to **oar**. So he settled on the **Marine Corps** to be first on foreign **shore**, as in the taking of **Corregidor**.

As cannons started to **roar** and bullets to **pour**, Georgie was slow to hit the **floor**, and one caught him smack in the **pos-te-ri-or**. So now he's back on our home **shore** knocking on Death's **door**.

Story 288

The Pirates of Yore

In the days of **yore**, pirates were feared on every **shore**. They wreaked suffering and **gore**, stealing silver and **stores** of other pre-cious **ores**.

In 1801 Thomas Jefferson became really **sore**. He called the Bar-ba-ry pirates "rotten to the **core**," and sol-emn-ly **swore** he'd settle the **score**. And this he did by an all-out **war**, ending it **forevermore**.

Story 289

A Sale No One Ignored

When wood dropped to $40 a **cord**, it was a price everyone could easily **afford**.

A **horde** of people came from every **ward**. Some ferried across a **fjord**. Others hopped **aboard** boats and **oared**. Everyone wanted as much as he could possibly **hoard**. However, woodsman **McCord** was able to **accord** each person just one **cord**.

Still all thanked the **Lord** and sang a joyous **chord**.

Story 290

The Settlers of New York

Most sailed on ships, but some floated on **corks**, while others were carried by long-winged **storks**.

Most came as farmers with a ready **pitchfork**, having plans to raise pigs for **pork**.

Yes--this is how it was for **Mork**, **O'Rourke**, and for all those other **York-ers** and **Corkers** who became our first **New Yorkers**.

Story 291

The Swarm

Now and then when the weather is fair and **warm** honey bees will **swarm**.

In their dress jacket **uniform**, they will **conform** to a box-shaped **form**. And when the Queen Bee's ready, she'll flap her wings to **inform** the workers that it's time to **perform**. Then they'll move her to another "**dorm**[1]."

1) A place to live.

Story 292

Hard As An Acorn

1. Do babies come **mother-born**, or **stork-borne**?
2. Should one **mourn** because it rains in the **morn**?
3. Is a bull's **horn** longer than a shoe **horn**?
4. Is a goose's **horn** louder than a French **horn**?
5. Is an ear of **corn** longer than **Cap-ri-corn**?
6. Is a goat **shorn** when its coat is too **worn**?

Story 293

Morse Code

The **source** of this dis-cov-er-y occurred when **Mrs. Morse** threatened her husband with **divorce**.

She took their one **horse** and moved to the opposite end of a golf **course**, surrounded by a thicket of **coarse** brambles and **gorse**.

At first Samuel planned to take her back by **force**, but he soon realized it was the wrong **course**.

Wanting so much to **discourse**, he yelled her name 'til he was **hoarse**. So, **perforce**, laying down a wire was his only **recourse**.

Story 294

Courting

If a boy has a sweetheart whom he would like to **court**, there are many things to do of the outdoor **sort** which will keep his money from running **short**.

He may visit an Army **fort**, or perhaps an **airport**. He may visit a **seaport** to watch ships that **transport exports** and **imports**.

But for most things, an **escort** needs his dad's **support**.

Story 295

Go North

By June **fourth**
Most people go **north**
Henceforth
The sun is fun
Only for those whose skin is **swarth**

OI

Story 296

Ship Ahoy!

As a baby, **Roy** brought his parents a lot of **joy**. **Mrs. Dubois** said she loved the way he acted **coy**, and how he played with a certain little **toy**.

She said, "He has never done anything to **annoy** me or **Mr. Dubois**, such as using a de-ceit-ful **ploy**. He has always been a great **joy**. And our pleasure will never **cloy**."

When **Roy** grew up he had to leave his home in **Illinois**. He joined the Navy's **employ** to be upon a ship in a **convoy** and fight the men of **Hanoi**.

His parents cau-tioned him to stay around a good **buoy**. Then they kissed their **boy** and said, "Ship **ahoy**, you dear, dear **Roy**!"

Story 297

Joyce

Joyce was the choir's **choice**
For so-pra-no **voice**
Her hymn
Made the cherubim in heaven **rejoice**

Story 298

Not To Be Foiled

Thanksgiving dinner was a thankless **toil**. The potatoes had to be cleaned of **soil**, the turkey wrapped in a-lu-mi-num **foil**, the salad mixed with vinegar and olive **oil**, and the gobbler put into the oven to **broil**.

Minutes after **Miss Doyle** put the potatoes in the water to **boil**, we discovered that our dinner plans would **spoil** because her oven had a broken heating **coil**.

Nevertheless, not a single guest minded the **turmoil** nor was the least bit **roiled**, for we all went to McDonald's and ate McChicken Sandwiches **royal**.

Story 299

Hard-Earned Coins

In summer a bricklayer might wear just a terry cloth around his **loins**, pinned together where one fold with the other **conjoins**.

On corners where one row of bricks and another **adjoin**, he alone must place a cornerstone called a **quoin**.

Now the heavy **quoin** might pull a muscle in his **groin**, but Local #1 of **Des Moines**--the union which he'd like to **join**--insists this be how he earn his **coin**.

Story 300

Girls and *Their Toys*

It's a well-known fact that little girls love little **boys**. Playing with **boys** is one of their favorite **joys**.

But if little girls make too much **noise** when bothering little **boys**, their mothers may lose their **poise** and make their daughters play with *other* ***toys***.

Story 301

Dad Rejoiced

Upon lazy Roy a job was **foist**, ir-re-spec-tive of the complaint he had **voiced**. He was made run a con-struc-tion **hoist**, and to carry many a fifty-pound **joist**.

Roy was sad, but his Dad was glad and he **rejoiced**.

a

Story 302

Back to the Scrub

Momma Bear and Poppa Bear wanted to join the Chicago **Cubs** Baseball **Club**. And so they did! However, in every game their team got **drubbed**. Thus it wasn't long before they found themselves benched, **dubbed scrubs**.

Having their hopes for stardom **snubbed**, Poppa Bear said to Momma Bear, "Let's return to the wild **scrub**." And so they did! There their life was much easier for-ag-ing for **grub**.

☞ See *Story 337*

Story 303

To Earn a Buck

To earn a **buck**:

A farmer needs to wallow in **muck** and sell corn in the **shuck** from the back of a **truck**.

A hunter needs patience to hunt the fleet-footed **buck** and the can-vas-back **duck**.

A pitcher needs to develop a fast **chuck**; and a hockey player, the skill to handle the **puck**.

Hence, anyone can earn a **buck**--provided he has **pluck** and drive to be other than a lazy **cluck**.

Story 304

A Product of "Ucts"

The kid was **ab-ducted**
The expense was **de-ducted**
The student was **in-structed**
The view was **ob-structed**
The building was **con-structed**
The soldier was **in-ducted**
The music was **con-ducted**
But the bank-rupt business was **mis-con-ducted**

Story 305

"The Dud"

Bud, please don't do this or that! **Bud's** mother would often cry. But **Bud** would reply, "Oh, **fuddy-dud**!"

Once **Bud** left on the spig-ot to pur-pose-ly cause a **flood**. At re-cess he could never catch on to **Spud**: whenever his number was called, instead of catch he'd **scud**.

His classmates said he acted like the Holly-wood super **stud**, **Hud**; that is, until one day when a pretty lass in his class hammered his nose and be-smeared his clothes with **blood**. Now instead of "**Bud**," everybody now calls him "**Dud**."

☞ See *Story 340*

Story 306

Ah Fudge!

"Ah **fudge**!" said the farmer
"My mule won't **budge**."
"Ah **fudge**!" said the pho-tog-ra-pher
"My photos got a **smudge**."
"Ah **fudge**!" said the factory worker
"My job's a **drudge**."
"Ah **fudge**! Uhm **fudge**!" said the fat lady
"Give me more of that sweet-tasting **fudge**."
"Ah **fudge**!" said the captain
"The river has too much **sludge**."
"Ah **fudge**!" said the criminal
"It's that same **judge**,
and no doubt he has a **grudge**."

Story 307

A Mere Powder Puff

Felicio was **tough** and no one gave the boy any **guff**.

Only he would dare to dive off the 100-foot **bluff**. In golf he never hit his ball into the **rough**, nor easy shots did he **fluff**. And in football, he was ex-treme-ly **rough**.

But when it came to his girl, who was hot **stuff** and much more than **enough**, he was a mere powder **puff**, and not the least bit **gruff**.

Story 308

Some "Ugs"

Trains **chug**
Boats **tug**
Shoulders **shrug**
Robbers **mug**
Fighters **slug**
And bears **hug**

Porters **lug**
Doctors **drug**
Jailors **jug**
Odors **fug**
Mosquitoes **bug**
Corks **plug** &
Guns **plug** too

☞ See *Story 342*

Story 309

Is It Love?

They fell in **love**. She kissed him and called him her "**turtle-dove**."

By and by, she convinced him that marriage would fit him like a **glove**.

But before he could ponder the con-se-quen-ces **thereof**, she gave him a **shove** to vow to the Lord **above**.

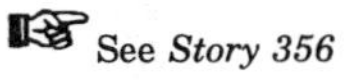

☞ See *Story 356*

This is truly the happiest day of your life!
Oh, nobody told me yet!

Story 310

The Lull Before The Storm

To **cull** his thoughts and **mull** over a certain problem, the man paddled his **scull** to sea. However, all he could see was an ever present **gull** (a **sea gull**), the blue sky, and the blue sea.

The sea died down, followed by a **lull**. Now the poor guy was **gulled** by this to think that the rest of the day would be **dull**.

But to his great surprise a storm followed the **lull** battering the boat's **hull** and shattering his thick **skull**.

Story 311

An Incredible Hulk

"John," said his angry mom, "as big as you are, whenever work is mentioned you always **sulk**, or you go out of sight and **skulk**, waiting 'til I'm through with the **bulk**.

"For sure--you're a very

'INCREDIBLE HULK!' "

Story 312

Judy Culp

Judy drinks water with a **gulp**
She drinks orange juice with the **pulp**
She wears coats of seal **sculp**
She molds clay into art **sculp**
She turns logs into "*paper*" **pulp** &
She turns words into "*worthless*" paperback **pulp**

Story 313

The Bum

In the city's **slum** in an alley behind a **gym-na-si-um**, there lives a **bother-some bum**. He begs for money, for say a **plum**, but usually buys **Bicardi Rum**. And he finds his food in a trash **drum**.

Once when offered a job selling **ge-ra-ni-ums** and **mums**, he out-right refused, citing **te-di-um** and a small pay **sum**.

Now he has no one with whom to **chum**, and he looks **glum**, for his life has **become** so **grum** and pa-thet-i-cal-ly **humdrum**.

☞ See *Story 346*

Story 314

Are You Dumb?

You are **dumb** if you don't know
the difference between go and **come**.
You are **dumb** if you don't know
the difference between all and **some**.
You are **dumb** if you don't know
your pinky from your **thumb**.
You are **dumb** if you don't know
a slice from a **crumb**.
You are **dumb** if you don't know
cockeyed from **plumb**.
You are **dumb** if you don't know
candy from **gum**.
And you are **dumb** if you don't know
sensitive from **numb**.

Story 315

Umpteen "Umps"

Bouncers **bump**
Clompers **clump**
Trucks **dump**
Grouches **grump**
Slouchers **slump**
Kan-ga-roos **jump**
Hikers **hump**

Windmills **pump**
Bruises **lump**
Ploppers **plump**
Cannons **thrump**
Officials **ump**
Drummers **thump**
Trumpeters **trump** &
Problems **stump**

Story 316

Attila The Hun

Attila the **Hun** was **one** of the most vi-cious men who ever lived under the **sun**. His enemies were **stunned** by the in-tri-cate traps he **spun**. With just a sword, never a **gun**, he fought just for **fun**.

Being fearful, even his own soldiers would **shun** "**The Hun**." But when he took Rome he hurt no **one**--not the Pope, not a priest, not a single **nun**--cer-tain-ly not a married **one**.

☞ See *Story 347*

Story 317

One To Won

Mr. Blevin said to his youngster, Kevin:

"Lesson **One**: **Anyone** and the hot **sun** can rise, but only the **sun** can set, **son**.

"Lesson TWO, I say to YOU: A **ton** of feathers weighs exactly the same as a **ton** of steel or a **ton** of anything except **fun**.

"Lesson Three, listen to me: Two take away **one** leaves **one**.

"Lesson Four, don't ignore: **One** take away **one** leaves absolutely **none**.

"Lesson Five's about wives: No **one** (no man, that is) should marry just **anyone**, and heavens never a **nun**!

"Lesson SIX will keep you from a FIX: Realize that what is well **begun** is nearly half **done**.

"And lastly, Lesson Seven, Kevin: Just because something *seems* lost, doesn't necessarily mean it can't be *found*--perhaps it can be **won**!"

☞ See *Story 216*

Story 318

The Dunce

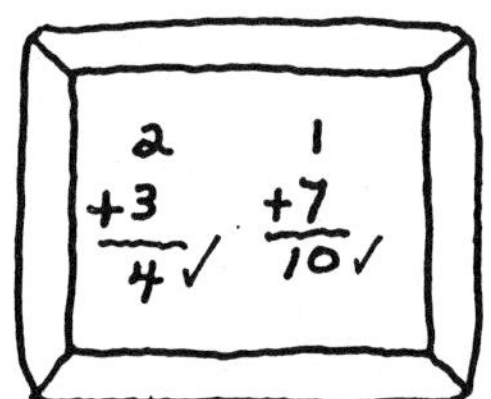

DUNCE
SOMEDAY I MIGHT WALK
ON THE MOON
WITH EINSTEIN!

Once a **dunce**, always a **dunce**
And a **dunce** doesn't know:
A pig **grunts**,
A tiger **hunts**,
A kicker **punts**,
Or that twice is double **once**.

Story 319

Punch

Mother said, "Children, because you ate a late **brunch**, it's my **hunch** that you're not yet hungry for your **lunch**.

"Later, 'though, you may be so; so if so you may have some **Hawaiian Punch**, a sandwich, and some potato chips on which to **munch** and **crunch**."

Story 320

The Song Was Moribund

The tenor was short and **ro-tund**
His face was red or **rub-i-cund**
His dress was tux with **cum-mer-bund**
His voice was pleasing and **or-o-tund**,
But his song was so sad and **mor-i-bund**
That the crowd cried "**REFUND**"

Story 321

The Ladder of "Ungs"

The song **sung**
The ball **flung**
The sharp **tongue**
And the hat **slung**

The bee **stung**
The batter **swung**
The vine **clung**
The spring **sprung**
And the bell **rung**

The human **lung**
The ladder **rung**
The cask **bung**
And the cow **dung**

The baby **young**
The rope **strung**
The picture **hung** &
The split jury **hung**

Story 322

The Plunge

The skin diver **plunged** into the water and speared a **muskellunge**, then she scooped up a big, live **sponge**.

Later for dinner she fried up the **muskellunge**, then she cleaned up with the now dried up **sponge**.

Story 323

No Bunk

There is:

The bed **bunk**
The bread **hunk**
The wood **chunk**
The soda **drunk**
The gooey **gunk**
The scrap **junk**
The cattail **punk**
And the wise **punk**

The colt's **spunk**
The elephant's **trunk**
The clothes **trunk**
The prayerful **monk**
The dumb **clunk**
The dull **clunk**
And the dull **plunk**

The water **dunk**
The basketball **dunk**
The foul **funk**
And the smelly **skunk**

Story 324

The "Drag" Bunt

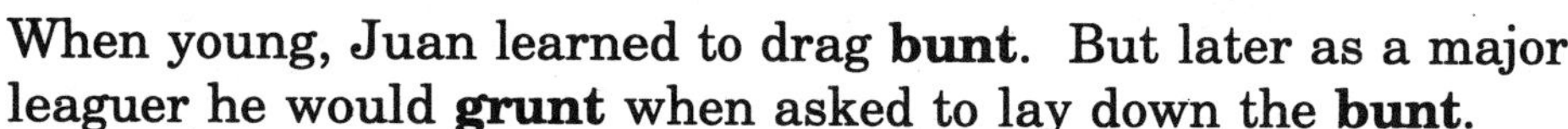

When young, Juan learned to drag **bunt**. But later as a major leaguer he would **grunt** when asked to lay down the **bunt**.

His thinking was that if the **brunt** of his hits were the mere **bunt**, he might as well quit his **hunt** to be in the game's **fore-front** and see his picture in every **store-front**.

Story 325

Hiccoughs Or Hiccups

When just a **pup** Jorge would **sup** his **supper** so fast that he would in-var-i-a-bly **hiccup**.

"Coke and Pepsi would just make him throw **up**! The only thing that worked was a **cup** of **7-Up**. Believe me--this is ain't no **gup**!"

Story 326

Gus Is Calamitous

As a waiter **Gus** wasn't a **plus**. He would cause a **fuss** and make the customers almost **cuss**.

Well, one day **Mr. Russ**, his boss, pulled him aside and said, "**Gus**, I'm **serious**, you're simply **ca-lam-i-tous**. You can't wait, and you can't **bus**. **Thus**, you'd best head out on the next **bus**. We have nothing further to **discuss**."

Story 327

Gushing

There is:

The carpet **plush**
The swanky **plush**
The food **mush**
The yell **mush**
And the lovers' **mush**

The snowy **slush**
And the garbage **slush**
The mad **rush**
And the fra-ter-ni-ty **rush**
The flat-ten-ing **crush**
And the lover's **crush**

The blooming **blush**
The embarrassed **blush**
And the cos-me-tic **blush**

The poker **flush**
The toilet **flush**
The wealthy **flush**
The river **flush**
And the door **flush**

The robin **thrush**
The quiet **hush**
The water **gush**
The hair **brush**
And the green **brush**

The green, green **lush**
The big, big **lush** &
The shouldn't **tush**, **tush**

Story 328

Poaching At Dusk

As night was setting in, **Officer Rusk** caught the poacher dead to rights with an elephant's **tusk** and the animal's **husk**.

The warden made him confess to having hunted oxen and deer for their fragrant **musk**. The poacher was fined and warned never, never again to hunt for **musk**, **tusk**, or **husk**, nor for any other game at or after **dusk**.

Story 329

Busting Out

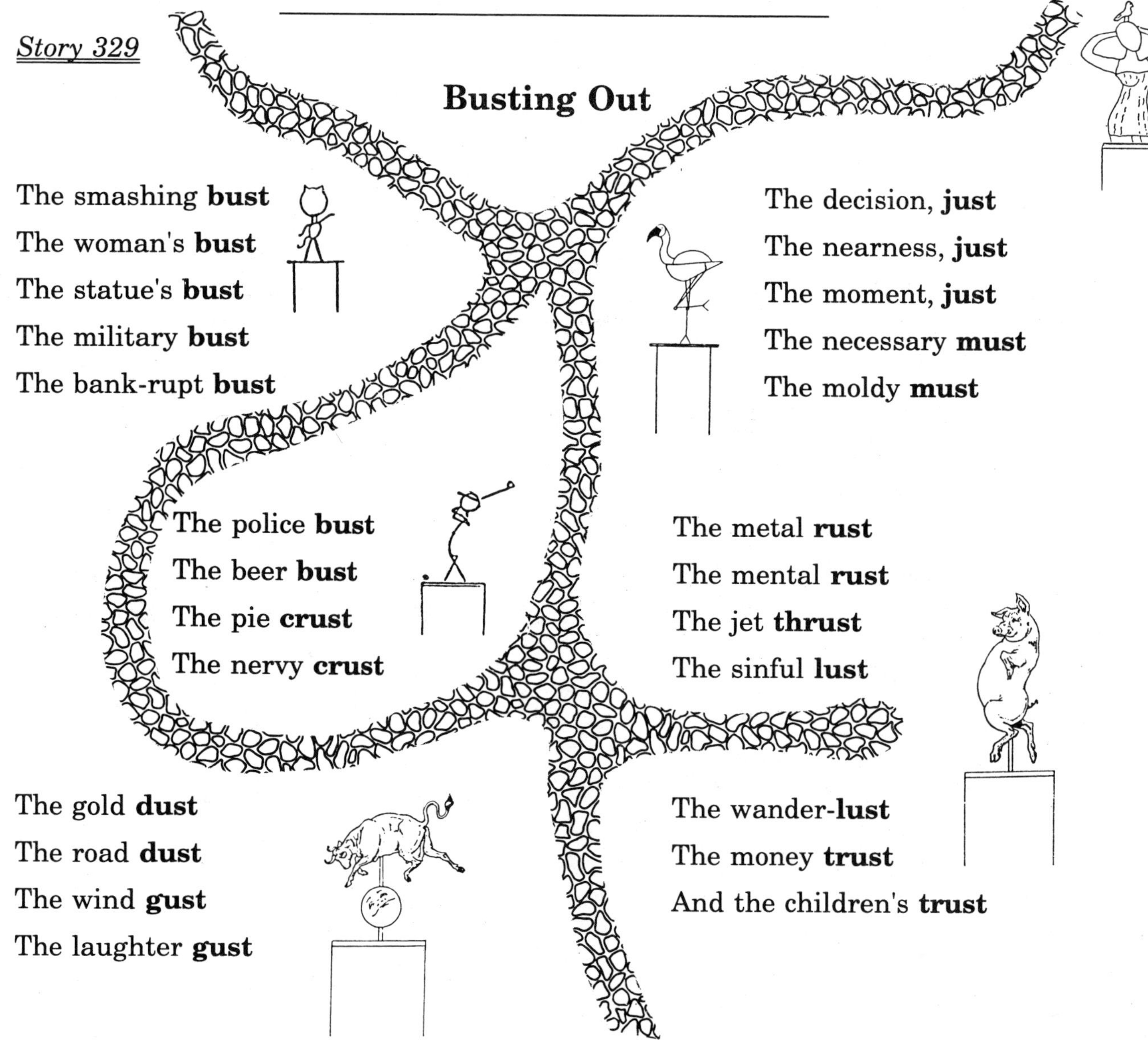

The smashing **bust**
The woman's **bust**
The statue's **bust**
The military **bust**
The bank-rupt **bust**

The decision, **just**
The nearness, **just**
The moment, **just**
The necessary **must**
The moldy **must**

The police **bust**
The beer **bust**
The pie **crust**
The nervy **crust**

The metal **rust**
The mental **rust**
The jet **thrust**
The sinful **lust**

The gold **dust**
The road **dust**
The wind **gust**
The laughter **gust**

The wander-**lust**
The money **trust**
And the children's **trust**

Story 330

From "But" All the Way to "What"

The **but** of the yes

The **butt** of the goat

The **butt** of the gun

The **butt** of the cigarette

The **butt** of the joke

The **cut** of the knife

The **cut** of the cloth

The **cut** of the insult

The **cut** of the runner

The **glut** of the glutton

The **glut** of the market

The **hut** of the woodsman

The **hut** of the quarterback

The **jut** of the cliff

The **mutt** of the kennel

The **mutt** of the class

The **nut** of the class

The **nut** of the squirrel

The **rut** of the mind

The **smut** of the chimney

The **smut** of the movies

The **shut** of the door

The **strut** of the rafter

The **strut** of the walker

The **putt** of the golfer

And the **putt-putt** of the motor

And the **tut-tut** of the scolder

☞ See *Story 350*

*Yo! So **what** happened to the "**what?**"*

Story 331

Study Much

There is:

A car's **clutch**
A hen's **clutch**
A large **clutch**
A gripping **clutch**
A coat **clutch**
A purse **clutch**
And a do-or-die **clutch**

A crotch **crutch**
A walking **crutch**
And a helpful **crutch**

A **Dutch** man
A **Dutch** uncle
A **Dutch** treat
And **Dutch** trouble

A rabbit **hutch**
A shack **hutch**
A furniture **hutch**

A so **much**
A too **much**
A very **much**
A frequent **much**
And a nearly **much**

A soiled **smutch**

Also, a degree **such**
And a nearly **such**
And a referring **such**
And a **such and such**

A light **touch**
A right **touch**
A woman's **touch**
A bordering **touch**
A sentimental **touch**
And, lastly,
A daffy **touch**

Story 332

The Confusing State of Flux

There are no **ducks** in a state of **flux**
There are no **trucks** in a state of **flux**
There are no **bucks** in a state of **flux**
Shucks! There is only an **influx**
Of big problems in a state of **flux**
And the central problem is at the **crux**

Story 333

From Buzz to Was

There is:

The bee **buzz**
The telephone **buzz**
And the gossipy **buzz**
The peach **fuzz**
The beard-like **fuzz**
And the police-type **fuzz**
The kissin' **coz**
The hubby **huz**
The verb **does**
The verb **was**
And the reason "just '**cause**"

U and OO

Story 334

Little Farmer Hugh

The **Carews** lived with their little **nephew**, **Hugh**. On their farm they had a ram, a **ewe**, and some other animals **too**.

Every morning the married **two** and **Hugh** would arise early feeling fresh and **new** as morning **dew**. **Mr. Carew** had a **slew** of odd jobs **to do**; such as, giving his horse a **new shoe**, or hunting ducks that overhead **flew**. **Mrs. Carew** had a lot **to do too**; such as, cooking **bar-be-cue**, or their favorite--duck **stew**. **Hugh**, he mostly had homework **to do** and lessons **to review**.

In church they prayed together at the same **pew**. And as their love for one another **grew**, God, in turn, blessed the pros-per-ous **two** and **nephew**, **Hugh**.

Story 335

Is It Not True?

Is it not **true** that the sky is **blue**? that rainbows have a multi-colored **hue**? that paste is no better than **glue**? that a hint is similar to a **clue**? that a **ewe** makes for tasty **ragout**? and that one may **sue** for money he believes his **due**?

Story 336

At The Zoo

"How **do you do**?" said the **cock-a-too**.
"**Coo-ku**," said the feathery **kuku**.
"**A-dieu**," said the **kan-ga-roo**
"**Moo**," said the cow--and the bull, **too**.
"**Coo**," said the pi-geons--both the **two**.
And "**Cockadoodledoo**," said **you** know **who**!

Story 337

A True Boob

Only a **boob** doesn't know that it takes water to make an ice **cube**, air to fill an **innertube**, and grease for a car **lube**.

And only a **boob** doesn't know that the six-sided **boob tube** is shaped like an ice **cube**.

☞ See *Story 302*

Story 338

The Little Pooch

The stray was an awfully big **mooch**
But the boy so loved his little **pooch**
That he built her a little **hooch**
For which she gave him a great big **smooch**

Story 339

Nailed to the Rood

During Lent, the priest ate very little **food**, and he kept in a con-tem-pla-tive **mood**.

Every day he went to church where he thought about Jesus being jeered and **booed**, then nailed to the **rood**. He thought of His great **for-ti-tude**, and he prayed for a life of **rec-ti-tude**.

☞ See *Story 358*

Story 340

Poor Gertrude

Gertrude and her parents began to **feud**. **Gertrude**, thinking she was so **shrewd**, left home wanting more **latitude** and took a job that was somewhat **lewd**.

"**Gertrude**," said a friend, "you have a terrible **attitude** and your dancing is awfully **crude**."

Gertrude responded, "You're plainly **rude**, a bit of a **prude**, and simply jealous of my **pul-chri-tude**."

As it turned out, poor **Gertrude** wasn't a bit **shrewd**: she married a no-good, do-nothing, **lewd**, jiving **dude**.

☞ See *Story 305*

Story 341

"Proofreading"

A clownish **goof**
A house **roof**
A mouth **roof**
A dog **woof**
A bull **woof**

A cow **hoof**
A distant **hoof**
A distant **aloof**
A photo **proof**
A legal **proof**
And a liquor **proof**

Story 342

The Stooge

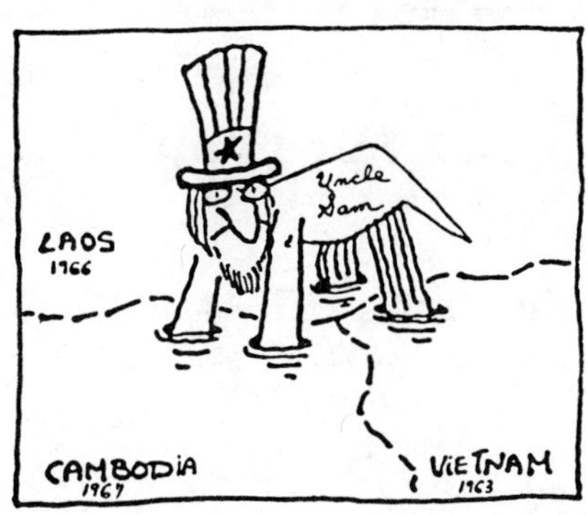

When the number of deaths in Viet Nam became **huge**, our President Nixon (1968-1974) could find no **refuge**.

We made him into our **stooge**. For everything, past and present, we crit-i-cized him in a **deluge**. We said he should have been more like a **Scrooge**. We said he wasted money and men and covered up with political **rouge** and **subter-fuge**.

☞ See *Story 308*

Story 343

Dimh Luk

Dimh Luk of Ha-noi, he no like be call' "**Dumb Kook**."

This badly an-noy **Luk**, though he not give no one no **rebuke**. To prove people w'ong, he learn to spell big word' like **Dubuque** an' **King Farouk**, an' he learn meaning of ot'er word like **fluke** an' **snook**.

Today no one **juke Luk**, for har' work has won **Dimh Luk** schol-ar-ship to **Baruch** and *n*other to U-ni-ver-si-ty **Duke**.

☞ See *Story 359*

Story 344

Food For Ghouls

When a subject breaks the King's **rule**, even though he may **mewl** or **pule**, he will be thrown in a dungeon unheated by **fuel**.

There he will be fed just soupy **gruel** and treated so ter-ri-bly **cruel**.

Later, when dead and his body **cool**, he then will be eaten by a blood-sucking **ghoul**.

Story 345

The "Precious" Jewel

Jewel was two when she quit dripping **drool**. At three she began swimming in the **pool**. At six she no longer feared the dentist's drilling **tool**.

At 13 she acted too "very **cool**" and broke nearly every **rule**. A year hence, however--when told she might flunk out of **school**--she quickly realized that all along she had been one big, ig-no-min-i-ous **fool**.

Story 346

The Bride and the Gloom

The bride felt like a beau-ti-ful blossom in **bloom**, for soon her fortune was about to **boom**. She was about to **assume**--perhaps totally **consume**--the wealth of her **groom**.

She was planning to spend lav-ish-ly on **perfume**, and to re-do his every **room**. She would **presume** to hire a maid in **costume** to **whom** to present with **broom** and **vacuum**.

The poor **groom** was soon to feel **gloom**. He would learn that big problems were going to **loom**. Sorely he felt the need for elbow **room**! He thought about getting into his car and **zoom**, but from the time in his mother's **womb**, somehow he knew of this in-ev-i-ta-ble **doom**. So instead, he would search for his soon-to-be **tomb**.

☞ See *Story 313*

Story 347

As The Band Crooned

In **June**, on a sand **dune**, under a full **moon**, a band called "**The Buffoons**" played a **looney tune** that made the **jejune** girls **swoon**.

Being en-rap-tured, **June** forgot her lunch of **prunes**. They were **soon** seen by a **raccoon**, a long-billed **loon**, and a **baboon**--who ate them properly with a **spoon**.

☞ See *Story 316*

Story 348

Rouen's Ruin

During World War II, the French city of **Rouen** was bombed and left in **ruin**.

For this and other bad things they were **doin'**, every German was called a "**bruin**."

Story 349

Fleeing The Coop

Tired of reporting the **poop**, the reporter decided to flee the "**coop**." So she sailed away in her 20-foot **sloop**.

But after just one Caribbean **loop**, however, her spirits began to **droop**. Then she realized she had been a **stupe**. So she sold her **sloop** and happily rejoined her old newspaper **group**.

Story 350

Their Guilt Is Moot

A "crazy **coot**" and a "big **galoot**" were ac-cused of stealing **loot**. The case was widely **bruited**. The public loudly **hooted**. The two they wanted **uprooted**.

In court, the judge asked the **brutes** with whom were they in **cahoots**, the whereabouts of the **loot**, and the reason they had to **shoot**. They answered, "We didn't need any **recruit** to help us spend the **loot**. And we don't give a **hoot** about winning this here **dispute**. Anything that we say you'll **refute** or at-tempt to **confute**."

The judge threatened that he would dress them in a zebra **suit** and **scoot** them off to jail by the shortest **route**. During court recess, however, they swal-lowed tainted (poi-son-ous) **fruit**. So whether they were actually guilty, is a question that will remain forever **moot**.

☞ See *Story 330*

Story 351

The Fuhrer Causes A Furor

Although Adolph Hitler was Germany's **Fuhrer**, his mind was in the **sewer**.

He said at once he wanted his country's e-co-nom-ic woes to **cure** and to make his A-ry-an race **pure**. So he devised the di-a-bol-i-cal plan to make another race **fewer**.

Con-se-quent-ly this started World War II by inciting the West into **furor**.

☞ See Stories *132 & 201*

Story 352

They Couldn't Endure

The wealthy Af-ri-can **Moor** and his pretty **par-a-mour** decided to take a **tour**. He **assured** his finicky **paramour** that their route would be straight and not have a winding hilly **contour**. However, they soon came upon a **detour** which took them through a **moor** on a road extremely **poor**.

At this she quickly said--"Please, let us quit this **detour**, I simply cannot **endure**!"

☞ See *Story 285*

Story 353

Vamoose

Big Chicken and his little **papoose** went a hunting for a **goose** in the marshes within a forest of **spruce**. But instead of finding a **goose**, they came upon an angry **moose**!

Big Chicken waved his white flag of **truce**, but red saw the charging **moose**. Luck, however, was theirs, for somehow they managed to break **loose** and . . . **VAMOOSE**!

Story 354

So Juiced

Drinking all day made **Mr. Proust** get so **juiced**. He would drink until his belt had to be **loosed**. Then he'd drink some more until he fell from his bar **roost**. Then there on the floor he'd say, "This is how I'm **used** . . . to giving my spirits a **boost**."

Story 355

Babe Ruth

As a **youth**, still without one front **tooth**, I used to watch the Yankees from a press-box **booth**. Though the New York crowd was at times a bit **uncouth**, I never had the slightest **ruth**. It was so much fun to see **Babe Ruth**. That's the honest-to-goodness **truth**!

Story 356

To The Louvre?

When Pierre made a false **move**, his teacher said: "Your behavior must **improve**! Your math, you always forget to **prove**, and your hat you never **remove**. Will you ever do anything of which I can **approve**? All I do is **reprove** and **disapprove**!

"Now, if you don't get into the **groove**, you'll be left behind when your class goes to the **Louvre**."

☞ See *Story 309*

Story 357

A Dishonorable Refusal

The idler **mused** over whether to join the Navy, but **refused**, fearing his talents would be **misused** and his body **abused**.

He said, "Sergeant, your promise to travel the world is just a **ruse**. Surely I would get an ocean **cruise**, but as to where I couldn't **choose**. Besides, Navy work is hard and I wouldn't get my daily afternoon **snooze**, and I hate G.I. 3.2 **booze**. And the Navy, having so many **do's** and don'ts, might cause me to blow my **fuse**, start a fight and even get a **bruise**. I'd seldom get hometown **news**, and before long I'd be singing the **blues**.

"Sorry, Sarge, but I'm not a bit **enthused**. Find someone with just a half a brain to **lose**, someone **who's** just *dying* to pay mortal **dues**."

Ŭ

Story 358

Misunderstood ?

"Sir, **could** you put some **wood** into my car's **hood**?" asked the woman, **Mrs. Wood**. "Certainly, Ma'am. Handling **wood** is my **livelihood**." he said.

"Well . . . then . . . why *don't* you?" barked **Mrs. Wood** in apt **womanhood**. He replied, "Do you mean **could**, or do you mean **would**?" "*Excuse me*!" she shouted, "*I do mean **would***!"

"Oh!" he responded, "I **would** as I said I **could**, but I don't think I really **should**. You see, your engine is already in your **hood**!"

At this she screamed,

"At once, Silly Boy, STOP THE F**OOLHARDIHOOD**!
I MEAN MY TRUNK AND NOT MY **HOOD**!
DO I MAKE MYSELF CLEARLY **UNDERSTOOD**?" ☞See *Story 339*

Story 359

Rooked

The fisherman watched as the trout hid in the **brook** under a rock in a little **nook**. It bit the bait and **took** the **hook**. Then it vi-o-lent-ly **shook**, though it couldn't **unhook**.

Later as the fisherman was taking a **look** at his **cookbook**, a sly **rook** swooped down and **took** the filleted **brook**.

The fisherman cried, "You common **crook**!"
And the bird replied--"You common **schnook**!"

☞ See *Story 343*

Story 360

The Bullfighter

It takes hardly any **pull**
Except the red cloth of **wool**
To en-rage the angry **bull**,
And to give the crowd its **full**.
They will yell, "How **wonderful**!
So ut-ter-ly **masterful**!"
In turn he'll show he's **thankful**
And bow and be so **graceful**

Story 361

Who's Pushy?

Ed said to his wife:

I do not like your hair--so **bushy**
I do not like your way--so **pushy**
And I do not like your words--so **mushy**
So, wife, being this is my one and only life,
Please--*do* try to make it a bit more **cushy**

NOTES ON USAGE

Anomalous Word: EXAMPLES--bar, car, war

Alternate Pronunciations: + EXAMPLES--sloth+, quay+

Underlined Lettering: a 2nd set of rhyming words

Shadowed Words: a 3rd set of rhyming words

Variant Spellings (within parentheses)

or: Equal or slightly less currency than first entry.

EXAMPLES--gray (*or* grey)
enplane (*or* emplane)

also: Considerably less currency than first entry

EXAMPLE--inflame (*also* enflame)

& or *and*: Makes no reference as to usage.

Within parentheses without *or* or *also*:

May show variant spelling without distinction as to currency of usage, or it may clarify pronunciation or give definition.

Abbreviations: noun n.
verb v.
adjective adj.
conjunction conj.

FAMILIES

Ă

Family 1	blab cab crab ☺ dab drab	Fab gab grab jab lab	nab scab slab stab tab	Arab
	(1)	(2)	(3)	(4)

Family 2	back black clack crack flack jack ☺ knack	lack pack quack rack sack shack slack	smack snack stack tack thwack track whack	pak flak (& flack) yak	claque plaque
	(1)	(2)	(3)	(4)	☺

Family 3	☺ act fact pact tract	re-act ex-act ex-tract	sub-tract im-pact in-ex-act
	(1)	(2)	(3)

Family 4	ad bad brad cad clad dad	fad gad glad had lad	mad ☺ pad sad shad tad	plaid	bade for-bade	add
	(1)	(2)	(3)	(4)	☺	(6)

*See Families 38 & 39

Family 5

(1)	(2)
badge	fadge
cadge	Madge

*See Family 152

Family 6

(1)	(2)	(3)	(4)	☺	(6)
gaff	calf	graph	laugh	gaffe	ca-rafe
chaff	half			☺ gi-raffe	
staff					

Family 7

(1)	(2)	(3)	(4)
aft	haft	waft	
craft	raft		daft (draught)
shaft			

Family 8

(1)	(2)	(3)	(4)	(5)
bag	flag ☺	nag	snag	zag
brag	gag	rag	stag	
crag	hag	sag	swag	
drag	jag	shag	tag	
fag	lag	slag	wag	

*See Family 41

Family 9

(1)	(2)		(4)	☺	(6)	(7)
am	dram	ma'am	sham	jamb	graham	jet-sam
bam	gram	Pam	slam	lamb		flot-sam
clam	ham	ram ☺	Spam		di-a-phragm	Mark-ham
cram	jam	yam	swam			
dam	lam	scam	tram		damn	
		scram	wham			

*See Family 45

Family 10

(1)	(2)	(3)
amp	lamp	tramp
camp	ramp	vamp
cramp	scamp	re-vamp
champ	stamp	
damp	tamp	

Family 11

an	fan	ran	Ann	Anne	woman
ban	Fran	scan			
bran	Jan	span			
can	man ☺	tan			
clan	pan	than			
Dan	plan	van			
(1)	(2)	(3)	(4)	☺	(6)

*See Family 47

Family 12

chance	prance	ants	am-bu-lance
dance	trance	pants	ig-no-rance
France	Vance		tol-er-ance
glance	en-hance		
lance	ad-vance		
Nance	ro-mance		
(1)	(2)	(3)	(4)

Family 13

blanch	ranch	Blanche
branch	stanch	av-a-lanche
flanch		
(1)	(2)	(3)

Family 14

and	hand	wand	Hol-land
band	land		Mary-land
bland	rand		
brand	sand		
gland	stand		
grand	strand		
(1)	(2)	(3)	(4)

Family 15

bang	pang	sprang	mer-ingue	har-angue
clang	rang	tang		
fang	sang	twang		
gang	slang	whang		
hang	spang	yang		
(1)	(2)	(3)	(4)	☺

*See Family 50

Family 16

bank	frank	shrank	franc	ankh
blank	lank	spank		
clank	plank	stank		
crank	prank	swank		
dank	rank	tank		
drank	sank	thank		
flank	shank	yank		
(1)	(2)	(3)	(4)	☺

Family 17

ant ☺	pant	☺	el-e-phant
cant	plant		Prot-es-tant
can't	rant		el-e-gant
chant	scant		
grant	shan't		
(1)	(2)		(3)

Family 18

cap	gap	pap	snap	yap
chap	knap	rap	strap	zap
clap	lap	sap	tap	
dap	map	scrap	trap	
flap	nap	slap	wrap	
(1)	(2)	(3)	(4)	☺

*See Family 52

Family 19

apse	re-lapse	Pabst
lapse	e-lapse	
		schnapps+
(1)	(2)	(3)

Family 20

apt	a-dapt	capped
rapt		gapped
wrapt		etc.
(1)	(2)	(3)

Family 21

ass	crass	Mass	gas	a-mass
bass	glass	mass		
brass	grass	☺ pass		
class	lass	sass		
(1)	(2)	(3)	(4)	☺

Family 22

ash	crash	hash	rash	po-tash	cache
bash	dash	lash	sash	suc-co-tash	pa-nache
brash	flash	mash	slash		mous-tache
cash	gash	Nash	smash		(& mus-tache)
clash	gnash	plash	stash		
(1)	(2)	(3)	(4)	☺	(6)

Family 23

ask	flask
bask	mask
cask	task
(1)	(2)

Family 24

chasm	has'em	sar-casm
spasm	pass'em	en-thu-si-asm
(1)	(2)	(3)

Family 25

asp	grasp	wasp
clasp	hasp	
gasp	rasp	
(1)	(2)	(3)

Family 26

blast	last	caste	asked
cast	mast		masked
fast	vast		etc.
(1)	(2)	(3)	(4)

Family 27				
	at	gnat	scat	swat
	bat	hat	slat	
	brat	mat	spat	what
	cat	pat	sprat	
	chat	plat	tat	
	fat	rat	that	
	flat	sat	vat	
	(1)	(2)	(3)	(4)

*See Family 54

Family 28					
	latch	match	scratch	snatch	watch
	catch	patch	slatch	thatch	swatch
	hatch	ratch	smatch		
	(1)	(2)	(3)	(4)	☺

*See Families 177, 220, 249, 275, 331, 338

Family 29		
	bath	path
	lath	wrath
	math	
	(1)	(2)

*See Family 56

Family 30			
	calve	have	valve
	halve		
	salve		
	(1)	(2)	(3)

Family 31		
	ax	tax
	flax	wax
	lax	re-lax
	Max	
	(1)	(2)

Family 32			
	as	La Paz	jazz
	has		razz
	(1)	(2)	(3)

Ā

Family 33

(1)	(2)	(3)	(4)	☺
bay	fray	lay	pray ☺	splay
bray	gay	May	quay+	spray
clay	gray (or grey)	may	ray	stay
day	hay	nay	say	stray
Fay	jay	pay	slay	sway
flay	Kay	play	spay	tray
				way

Family 34

(1)	(2)	(3)	(4)
fey	fil-let	cro-chet	ex-po-sé
lea (*or* ley)	(*also* filet)	bou-quet	(*or* ex-po-se)
prey	sa-chet		
they	ri-co-chet		
trey	Chev-ro-let		
whey			
heigh (*or* hey)			

Family 35

(1)	(2)	(3)	(4)	☺
heigh (or hey)	Ca-lais	neg-li-gee	par-fait	Raleigh
neigh	Bor-de-lais	mat-i-nee		
sleigh		soi-ree		
weigh		pro-te-gee (*f.*)		
				lei
		pro-te-ge (*male*)		

Family 36

(1)	(2)	(3)
ace	pace	em-brace
brace	place	dis-grace
face	race	dis-place
grace	space	
lace	trace	
mace		

Family 37

(1)	(2)	(3)
base	☺ vase	pur-chase
case	en-case	
chase	de-base	

Family 38

(1)	(2)	(3)	(4)	☺
ade	lade	a-brade	suede	per-suade
blade	made	ar-cade		dis-suade
fade	shade	e-vade		
glade	spade	ti-rade		
grade	trade	gre-nade		
jade	wade			

*See Family 4

Family 39

(1)	(2)	(3)
aid	paid	aide
braid	raid	
laid	staid	
maid ☺		

Family 40

(1)	(2)	(3)
chafe	un-safe	waif
safe		
strafe		

Family 41

(1)	(2)	(3)	(4)
age	sage	gauge (*or* gage)	en-cage
cage	stage		en-gage
page	swage		en-rage
rage	wage		

*See Families 152 & 223

Family 42

(1)	(2)	(3)	(4)	☺	(6)	(7)
bake	fake	lake	sake	stake	a-wake	sheik+
brake	flake	make	shake	take	re-take	
cake	hake	quake	slake	wake	re-make	ache
drake	Jake	rake	snake			

Family 43

ale	kale	shale	re-sale
bale	male	stale	fe-male
dale	pale	swale	
gale	rale	tale	
hale	sale	whale	
	scale	vale	
(1)	(2)	(3)	(4)

Family 44

ail	frail	mail	sail	braille	re-tail	veil
bail	Gail	nail	snail		re-mail	un-veil
brail	Grail	pail	tail			re-nail
fail	hail	quail	trail			de-rail
flail	jail	rail	wail			
(1)	(2)	(3)	(4)	☺	(6)	(7)

Family 45

blame	fame	lame	re-name
came	flame	name	un-tame
dame	game	same	en-frame
		shame	in-flame
		tame	(*also* enflame)
(1)	(2)	(3)	(4)

*See Family 9

Family 46

aim	ex-claim
claim	dis-claim
maim	re-claim
(1)	(2)

Family 47

bane	mane	Maine	in-sane
cane	pane		en-plane
crane	plane		(*or* emplane)
Dane	sane		in-ane
Jane	vane		
lane	wane		cham-pagne
(1)	(2)	(3)	(4)

*See Family 11

Family 48

(1)	(2)	(3)	(4)	(5)
brain	lain	sprain	en-chain	cam-paign
Cain	main	stain	in-grain	
chain	pain	strain	re-gain	
drain	plain	swain	re-frain	
fain	rain	train	re-sprain	
gain	slain	twain	re-train	
grain	Spain	vain	re-main	

Family 49

(1)	(2)	(3)	(4)
mein	deign	seine	Duquesne
rein	feign		
vein	reign		

Family 50

(1)	(2)	(3)
change	ex-change	flange
mange	re-ex-change	
range	un-change	
strange		

*See Family 15

Family 51

(1)	(2)	(3)	(4)
faint	saint	ain't	feint
paint	taint		
quaint	re-straint		

Family 52

(1)	(2)	(3)	(4)
ape ☺	jape	crepe	a-gape
cape	nape		es-cape
crape	scrape		re-shape
drape	shape		
gape	tape		
grape			

*See Family 18

Family 53

baste	taste	waist	caste
haste	waste		
paste			
(1)	(2)	(4)	(5)

Family 54

ate	gate	mate	sate	fete	a-bate	ac-cu-rate
bate	grate	pate	skate		de-bate	mod-er-ate
crate	hate	plate	slate		re-bate	es-ti-mate
date	Kate	prate	spate		e-late	for-tu-nate
fate	late	rate	state		re-late	
					in-grate	
(1)	(2)	(3)	(4)	☺	(6)	(7)

*See Family 27

Family 55

bait	strait	straight	eight	height
gait	trait		freight	sleight
plait	wait		weight	
(1)	(2)	(3)	(4)	(5)

Family 56

bathe	scathe
lathe	swathe+
(1)	(2)

*See Family 29

Family 57

brave	grave	shave	be-have	waive	suave
cave	knave	slave	en-grave		
crave	nave	stave	re-pave		
Dave	pave	wave			
gave	rave				
(1)	(2)	(3)	(4)	☺	(6)

Family 58

blaze	faze (& phase)	graze	a-blaze
braze	gaze	haze	a-maze
craze	glaze	laze	
daze		maze	
		raze	
(1)	(2)	(3)	(4)

Family 59				
	braise (& braize)		baize	phase
	chaise		maize	phrase
	praise			re-phrase
	raise			
		re-praise		
		up-raise		
	(1)	(2)	(3)	(4)

AR

Family 60					
	bar	par	war	gui-tar	cir-cu-lar
	car	scar			reg-u-lar
	czar	spar		ca-tarrh	sim-i-lar
	far	star			
	jar	tar			
	mar	ajar			
	(1)	(2)	(3)	(4)	☺

See Family 74

Family 61		
	Barb	rhu-barb
	Darb	
	garb	
	(1)	(2)

Family 62			
	arch	parch	mon-arch
	larch	starch	
	march		
	(1)	(2)	(3)

Family 63				
	bard	lard	guard	leo-pard
	card	shard		lan-yard
	hard	yard		
	(1)	(2)	(3)	(4)

Family 64			
	arf	dwarf	scarf
	barf	wharf	(*or* scarph, *a joint*)
	scarf (garment)		
	(1)	(2)	(3)

Family 65			
	barge	Marge	en-large
	charge	parge	
	large	Sarge	
	(1)	(2)	(3)

Family 66					
	ark ☺	lark	arc	aard-vark	New-ark+
	bark	mark			
	cark	park			
	dark	shark			
	hark	stark			
	(1)	(2)	(3)	(4)	☺

Family 67			
	Carl	quarrel	laurel+
	gnarl		
	snarl		sorrel+
	(1)	(2)	(3)

Family 68			
	arm ☺	warm	a-larm
	charm		re-arm
	farm		dis-arm
	harm		
	(1)	(2)	(3)

Family 69			
	barn	tarn	bairn (*or* barn)
	carn	yarn	cairn (*or* carn)
	darn		
	(1)	(2)	(3)

Family 70

(1)	(2)	(3)
carp	sharp	warp
harp	tarp	

Family 71

(1)	(2)
arse	farce
parse	sparse (*also* sparce)

Family 72

(1)	(2)	(3)	(4)
art	dart	part	heart
cart	hart	smart	♥
chart	part	start	
		tart	

Family 73

(1)	(2)	(3)
carve	starve	Marv
		Harve

ĀR̃

Family 74

(1)	(2)	(3)	(4)
bare	glare	share	a-ware
blare	hare ☺	snare	be-ware
care	mare	stare	una-ware
dare	pare	square	com-pare
fare	rare	tare	pre-pare
flare	scare	ware	en-snare

*See Family 60

Family 75

(1)		(3)	(4)	(5)
☺ bear	for-bear (*to refrain*)	there	they're	heir
pear	fore-bear (*an ancestor or forbear*)	where		their
tear		no-where	Cher	weir+
wear		any-where		
swear		some-where	err	

*See Family 129

Family 76

air	flair	lair	un-fair	re-pair
chair	glair	pair	af-fair	dis-re-pair
fair	hair	stair	im-pair	de-spair
(1)	(2)	(3)	(4)	(5)

Ĕ

Family 77

bleb	neb	ebb
Feb	reb	
Jeb	web	
deb		
(1)	(2)	(3)

Family 78

beck	☺ neck	Czech	trek	Que-bec
check	peck	Tech		
deck	reck			
fleck	speck			
heck	wreck			
(1)	(2)	(3)	(4)	☺

Family 79

sect	di-rect	per-fect	in-ter-ject	re-elect
dis-sect	in-di-rect	pre-fect	ob-ject	se-lect
in-sect	mis-di-rect	de-fect	pro-ject	in-tel-lect
in-ter-sect	e-rect	gen-u-flect	re-ject	di-a-lect
col-lect	res-ur-rect	in-flect	sub-ject	pro-spect
rec-ol-lect	af-fect	re-flect	de-tect	re-spect
con-nect	de-fect	ab-ject	pro-tect	dis-re-spect
dis-con-nect	ef-fect	de-ject	ar-chi-tect	cir-cum-spect
cor-rect	in-vect	e-ject	ne-glect	in-tro-spect
in-cor-rect	per-fect	in-ject	e-lect	re-tro-spect
(1)	(2)	(3)	(4)	☺

Family 80

bed	red	said	bread	tread	in-stead
bled	shed		dead	thread	bed-stead
bred	shred		dread		home-stead
fed	sled		head		
fled	sped		lead		
Fred	ted		read		
led	Ted		stead		
Ned	pled		spread		
(1)	(2)	(3)	(4)	☺	(6)

*See Family 107

Family 81

dredge	ledge	knowl-edge	sac-ri-lege+
edge	pledge		
fledge	sedge		
hedge	sledge		
kedge	wedge		
(1)	(2)	(3)	(4)

Family 82

eft		ef	
eft	left	chef	deaf
cleft	theft	clef	
deft	weft	ref	
heft	bereft		
(1)	(2)	(3)	(4)

Family 83

beg ☺	peg	egg	Craig	Hague
dreg	skeg	yegg		vague
keg	teg			plague
leg				
Meg				
(1)	(2)	(3)	(4)	☺

Family 84

bell	jell	snell	retell	re-bel	mo-tel
cell	knell	spell	befell	ex-pel	la-pel
dell	quell	swell		com-pel	cara-mel
dwell	sell	well		im-pel	
fell	shell	yell		re-pel	
hell	smell			ho-tel	
(1)	(2)	(3)	(4)	☺	(6)

Family 85

elch	eld	☺ elf	elm	elp
belch	geld	elf	elm	help
squelch	held	delf	helm	kelp
Welch+	meld	self	whelm	skelp
(*or* Welsh)	weld	shelf	realm	whelp
	up-held			yelp
(1)	(2)	(3)	(4)	(5)

Family 86

belt	melt	dealt	svelte	mis-spelt
Celt	pelt		(& svelt)	
dwelt	smelt			
felt	spelt			
gelt	welt			
(1)	(2)	(3)	(4)	☺

Family 87

elth		elve
health	twelfth+	delve
wealth		helve
stealth		shelve
		twelve
(1)	(2)	(3)

Family 88

Clem	mayhem	con-demn	phlegm
gem	requiem	con-temn	ap-o-thegm
hem	di-a-dem		(*or* ap-o-phthegm)
them			
stem			
(1)	(2)	(3)	(4)

Family 89	tempt kempt	dreamt	at-tempt con-tempt pre-empt	ex-empt un-kempt
	(1)	(2)	(3)	(4)

Family 90	den fen glen hen ken men	pen ten then when wren yen	can+ a-gain+	☻ Af-ri-can A-mer-i-can
	(1)	(2)	(3)	(4)

Family 91

fence hence thence	cense dense sense	of-fense de-fense sus-pense	ex-pense in-tense in-cense	def-er-ence dif-fer-ence con-se-quence com-mence
(1)	(2)	(3)	(4)	(5)

Family 92	bench blench clench drench flench French	quench stench tench trench wench wrench	en-trench
	(1)	(2)	(3)

Family 93

bend blend end fend lend mend rend	send spend tend trend vend wend	friend befriend at-tend of-fend pre-tend a-mend e-mend	as-cend de-scend de-pend in-tend con-tend com-mend ex-tend	de-fend dis-tend	ap-pre-hend com-pre-hend rec-om-mend
(1)	(2)	(3)	(4)	☺	(6)

Family 94

bent	sent	in-tent	ac-cent	el-e-phant+
cent	scent	e-vent	con-tent	ig-no-rant+
dent	tent	ab-sent	in-vent	tol-er-ant+
gent	Trent	in-dent	dis-sent	ju-bi-lant+
Ghent	sprent	re-pent	con-vent	oc-cu-pant+
Kent	stent	re-sent	pre-vent	con-ver-sant+
lent	vent	ad-vent	re-lent	
pent	went	de-scent	com-pe-tent	
		as-sent	ac-ci-dent	
	meant	as-cent	in-ci-dent	
		res-i-dent		
(1)	(2)	(3)	(4)	☺

Family 95

crept	a-dept	in-ter-cept	leapt
kept	ac-cept		
slept	ex-cept		
swept	in-ept		
wept			
(1)	(2)	(3)	(4)

Family 96

Bess	less	yes	guess	im-press
bless	mess			ex-press
chess	press			de-press
cress	stress			com-press
dress	tress			re-cess
fess				ab-scess
(1)	(2)	(3)	(4)	(5)

Family 97

flesh	en-mesh	creche+
fresh		
mesh		
thresh		
(1)	(2)	(3)

Family 98

best	jest	test	guest	con-test	breast
blest	lest	vest	quest	in-vest	
chest	nest	west		di-vest	
crest	pest	wrest		at-test	
fest	rest	zest		be-hest	
				ar-rest	
(1)	(2)	(3)	(4)	(5)	(6)

Family 99

bet	met	stet	a-bet	bru-nette	threat
fret	net	vet	re-set	An-nette	sweat
get	pet	wet	as-set	Clau-dette	
jet ☺	ret	whet	be-set	Gill-ette	debt
let	set	yet	ca-det	Cor-vette	
				ban-quette	vi-o-let
				et-i-quette	com-et
(1)	(2)	(3)	(4)	☺	(6)

Family 100

etch	retch	catch+
fetch	sketch	
fletch	stretch	
ketch	vetch	
letch	wretch	
(1)	(2)	(3)

Family 101

death	Beth	MacBeth	twentieth+
breath	Seth	Elizabeth	thirtieth+
(1)	(2)	(3)	(4)

*See Families 125 & 126

Family 102

flex	sex	an-nex	next	pre-text
hex	Tex	con-vex	text	con-text
kex	vex	re-flex	sext	
prex		per-plex		
rex		com-plex		
(1)	(2)	(3)	(4)	(5)

Ē

Family 103

be	bee	ghee	spree	a-gree	Mary	very	Marie
he	Cree	glee	tee	disagree			Rosalie
me	fee	knee	thee	de-cree	marry		
she	flee	lee	three	tee-pee	carry		esprit
we	free	see	tree				
ye	gee	scree	wee	ante			
(1)	(2)	(3)	(4)	(5)	☺	(7)	☺

Family 104

pea	plea	key	de-bris	en-nui	ski
flea	sea				
lea+(& ley)	tea				
(1)	(2)	(3)	(4)	(5)	☺

Family 105

beech	be-seech	each	peach
breech	un-breech	beach	preach
breech(es)+		bleach	reach
leech		breach	teach
screech		leach	im-peach
speech			
(1)	(2)	(3)	(4)

Family 106

bleed	greed	steed	ex-ceed	con-cede	im-pede
breed	heed	screed	pro-ceed	re-cede	cen-ti-pede
creed	meed	teed	mis-deed	se-cede	mil-li-pede
deed	need	treed	suc-ceed	ac-cede	cede
feed	seed	tweed		pre-cede	glede
freed	speed	weed			Swede
(1)	(2)	(3)	(4)	(5)	(6)

Family 107

bead	mead	super-sede
knead	plead	(*or* supercede)
lead	read	
(1)	(2)	(3)

*See Family 80

Family 108

league	fa-tigue	re-nege+
col-league	in-trigue	
(1)	(2)	(3)

Family 109

beef	leaf	brief	be-lief	grief	mis-chief
reef	sheaf	chief	re-lief	lief	hand-ker-chief
		fief		thief	
		dis-be-lief			
(1)	(2)	(3)	(4)	(5)	☺

Family 110

cheek	meek	eke	chic	shriek	sheik+
cleek	peek	Zeke			
creek	reek				
gleek	seek				
Greek	sleek				
leek	week				
(1)	(2)	(3)	(4)	(5)	(6)

Family 111

beak	peak	teak	Ches-a-peake	clique+	steak
bleak	sneak	tweak		an-tique	
creak	speak	weak		o-blique	
freak	squeak	wreak		pique	
leak	streak			Mo-nique	
				phy-sique	
(1)	(2)	(3)	(4)	(5)	☺

Family 112

eel	peel	Lu-cille	spiel	Neil	Cas-tile
feel	reel	Ca-mille	schemiel		au-to-mo-bile
heel	seel	Bas-tille			
keel	steel				
kneel	wheel				
	genteel				
(1)	(2)	(3)	(4)	(5)	(6)

Family 113

(1)	(2)	(3)	(4)	(5)
deal	seal	weal	ap-peal	con-geal
heal	squeal	wheal	re-peal	con-ceal
meal	steal	zeal	an-neal	re-veal
peal	teal		sur-real	com-mon-weal
real	veal			

Family 114

(1)	(2)	(3)	(4)
field	weald	afield	heeled
shield			keeled
wield			reeled
yield			etc.

Family 115

(1)	(2)	(3)
beam	ream	in-seam
bream	seam	ice cream
cream	scream	
dream	steam	
fleam	stream	
gleam	team	

Family 116

(1)	(2)	(3)
deem	theme	re-gime
seem	scheme	
teem	ex-treme	
re-deem	su-preme	
es-teem	blas-pheme	
	ac-a-deme	

Family 117

(1)	(2)	(3)	(4)	(5)
bean	lean	un-clean	co-deine	mesne
clean	mean	de-mean	caf-feine	de-mesne+
dean	quean			
glean	wean	stean		
Jean	yean	(*or* steen)		
		steen		
		(*or* stein, steyn)		

Family 118

been+	seen	ca-reen	scene	lien	rou-tine
green	screen	Ka-reen	ob-scene	mien	ma-chine
keen	sheen	Mau-reen	Eu-gene		vas-e-line
peen	spleen	be-tween	I-rene		nic-o-tine
preen	teen	can-teen	se-rene		nec-tar-ine
queen	thir-teen	ker-o-sene			mag-a-zine
					gas-o-line
(1)	(2)	(3)	(4)	(5)	☺

Family 119

cheep	seep	a-sleep
creep	sheep	
deep	sleep	
jeep	steep	
keep	sweep	
peep	weep	
(1)	(2)	(3)

Family 120

heap	leap
reap	neap
(1)	(2)

Family 121

cease	Nice	o-bese	fleece	niece	ce-rise	de-crease
crease	Ber-nice		Greece	piece	va-lise	de-cease
grease	Mau-rice	Reese		a-piece		re-lease
lease	po-lice		peace	ca-price		
(1)	(2)	(3)	(4)	(5)	☺	(7)

*See Family 128

Family 122

beast	feast	priest	breast
east	least		
	yeast		
(1)	(2)	(3)	(4)

Family 123

(1)	(2)	(3)	(4)
eat	meat	de-feat	great
beat	neat	up-beat	
bleat	peat	re-treat	
cleat	seat	un-seat	
cheat	treat	mis-treat	
feat	wheat		
heat			

Family 124

(1)	(2)	(3)	(4)	(5)	☺
beet	sheet	dis-creet	Crete	de-lete	de-ceit
feet	skeet	par-a-keet	mete	ath-lete	con-ceit
fleet	sleet		Pete	re-plete	
greet	street	suite	com-pete	dis-crete	re-ceipt
meet	sweet		de-plete		e-lite

Family 125

(1)	(2)	(3)	(4)
heath	beneath	teeth	Keith
sneath	underneath		Leith
sheath	bequeath		
	wreath		

*See Family 101

Family 126

(1)	(2)
breathe	seethe
sheathe (*v.*)	teethe
wreathe (*v.*)	

*See Family 101

Family 127

(1)	(2)	(3)	(4)	(5)	☺
eave	keeve (*or* kieve)	eve	we've	grieve	naive
cleave	reeve	breve		thieve	per-ceive
heave	sleeve	Steve		be-lieve	con-ceive
leave	steeve			re-lieve	de-ceive
sheave				re-prieve	re-ceive
sleave				re-trieve	ag-grieve

Family 128

ease	sleaze	frieze	seize	fees	breeze
grease(*v.*)				lees	freeze
please				sees	sneeze
tease	these	Louise			squeeze
ap-pease		bise			tweeze
dis-ease					wheeze
(1)	(2)	(3)	(4)	(5)	(6)

*See Family 121

ĒR̃

Family 129

beer	peer	ca-reer	mere	ear	rear	bier
cheer	queer	pi-o-neer	here	blear	sear	pier
deer ☺	seer	en-gi-neer	sere	clear	shear	tier
fleer	sheer	dom-i-neer	sphere	dear	smear	cash-ier
jeer	sneer	buc-ca-neer	ad-here	drear		fron-tier
leer	steer		co-here	fear	tear	
	veer			gear	year	
		hem-i-sphere		hear	spear	
		sou-ve-nir				
	(2)	(3)	(4)	(5)	☺	(7)

*See Family 75

Family 130

☺ fierce
pierce
tierce
(1)

Family 131

beard	weird	feared
		neared
(1)	(2)	(3)

R̃

Family 132

(1)	(2)	(3)	(4)	(5)	(6)	(7)	(8)
blur	purr	fir	in-cur	in-ter	a-ver	pop-u-lar	her
bur	burr	sir	oc-cur	de-ter	in-fer		per
cur		stir	con-cur	mus-ter	con-fer		
fur	were	astir	re-cur	en-ter	re-fer	in-jure	
slur		bestir		in-ter	de-fer	chirr	
spur		whir		pre-fer	myrrh		

*See Families 201 & 351

Family 133

(1)	(2)	(3)
gerb	blurb	ad-verb
Herb	curb	su-perb
herb	dis-turb	
verb	per-turb	
	sub-urb	
	ex-urb	

Family 134

(1)	(2)	(3)	(4)
birch	church	perch	search
smirch	lurch	re-search	
be-smirch			

Family 135

(1)	(2)	(3)	(4)	(5)	☺
bird	curd	herd	heard	word	on-ward
gird	turd	nerd	over-heard		up-ward
third	surd		Byrd		
etc.					
	ab-surd				

Family 136

(1)	(2)	(3)
turf	serf	Murph
surf	kerf	
scurf		

Family 137

merge	gurge	dirge	scourge	e-merge
verge	purge			di-verge
serge	surge			con-verge
	urge			sub-merge
	spurge			im-merge
	splurge			
(1)	(2)	(3)	(4)	(5)

Family 138

clerk	irk	shirk	lurk	work	Burke	cirque
jerk	chirk	smirk	murk			
perk	quirk	stirk	Turk			
(1)	(2)	(3)	(4)	(5)	☺	(7)

Family 139

burl	hurl	girl ☺	earl	whorl
curl	knurl	swirl	pearl	
churl	purl	skirl		
furl	thurl	twirl		
	whirl			
(1)	(2)	(3)	(4)	(5)

Family 140

berm (*or* berme)	firm	worm	in-firm	dis-af-firm
derm	squirm		af-firm	
germ			con-firm	mis-term
sperm			re-af-firm	pach-y-derm
term				
(1)	(2)	(3)	(4)	(5)

Family 141

urn	Bern	earn	ad-journ	re-turn	con-cern
burn	fern	learn	so-journ	up-turn	dis-cern
churn	quern	yearn		tac-i-turn	a-stern
spurn	stern				in-tern
turn	tern		erne		
			(*or* ern)		
(1)	(2)	(3)	(4)	(5)	(6)

Family 142

(1)	(2)	(3)
burp	chirp	twerp
slurp		Ant-werp
u-surp		

Family 143

(1)	(2)	(3)	(4)	(5)	☺
curse	hearse	worse	terse	a-verse	in-verse
nurse	re-hearse		verse	ad-verse	di-verse
purse				re-verse	per-verse
dis-burse				con-verse	dis-perse

Family 144

(1)	(2)	(3)	(4)
blurt	dirt	pert	de-sert
curt	flirt	a-lert	des-sert
hurt	girt	a-vert	in-vert
spurt (*also* spirt)	shirt	ad-vert	ex-pert
	skirt	re-vert	ex-ert
	squirt		

Family 145

(1)	(2)	(3)	(4)	(5)
berth	birth	earth	worth	Furth
Perth	firth	dearth		
	girth	hearth		
	mirth			

Family 146

(1)	(2)	(3)	(4)
burst	first	Hearst	worst
hurst	thirst		

Family 147

(1)	(2)	(3)	(4)
nerve	curve	ob-serve	de-serve
serve		un-nerve	con-serve
swerve		re-serve	pre-serve
		verve	

Ĭ

Family 148

bib	fib	lib	sib
crib	glib	nib	squib
dib	jib	rib	
(1)	(2)	(3)	(4)

*See Family 189

Family 149

brick	lick	slick	Cath-o-lic
chick	nick	snick	lu-na-tic
click	pick	stick	a-rith-me-tic
crick	prick	thick	
flick	quick	tick	
hick	Rick	trick	
kick	sick	wick	
(1)	(2)	(3)	(4)

Family 150

pict	e-vict	der-e-lict	in-dict
strict	con-flict	in-ter-dict	
ad-dict	in-flict	de-pict	
af-flict	pre-dict	re-strict	
(1)	(2)	(3)	(4)

Family 151

id	kid	Sid	aid	liq-uid
bid	lid	skid		or-chid
did	mid	squid ☺		
grid	quid			
hid	rid			
(1)	(2)		(4)	(5)

*See Family 191

Family 152

bridge	cab-bage	spin-ach	mar-riage
midge	sau-sage		
ridge	pil-grim-age		
smidge	voy-age		
(1)	(2)	(3)	(4)

*See Families 5, 41 & 223

Family 153					
	cliff miff riff skiff	sniff stiff tiff whiff	if	griffe	glyph
	(1)	(2)	(3)	(4)	(5)

*See Family 193

Family 154			
	drift gift lift	rift shift shrift	sift swift thrift
	(1)	(2)	(3)

Family 155				
	big brig dig fig	gig grig jig mig	☺ pig prig rig spig	sprig swig twig Whig
	(1)	(2)	(3)	(4)

Family 156				
bill brill chill dill drill fill	frill gill grill hill ill kill	mill pill shill shrill still swill thrill	till (*also* til *prep & conj*) till (*verb & noun*) krill trill twill will	'til nil un-til re-fill
(1)	(2)	(3)	(4)	(5)

Family 157		
	filch milch	pilch zilch
	(1)	(2)

Family 158		
	build guild	gild
	(1)	(2)

Family 159		
	ilk bilk	milk silk
	(1)	(2)

Family 160

gilt	silt	built	re-built
hilt	spilt	guilt	
jilt	stilt	quilt	
kilt	tilt		
milt	wilt		
(1)	(2)	(3)	(4)

Family 161

brim	Jim	slim	limb	hymn	an-to-nym
dim	Kim	swim			hom-o-nym
glim	prim	Tim	limn	gym	syn-o-nym
grim	rim	trim			
him	skim	vim			
		whim			
(1)	(2)	(3)	(4)	(5)	☺

*See Family 197

Family 162

imp	gimp	scrimp
blimp	limp	shrimp
crimp	primp	skimp
(1)	(2)	(3)

Family 163

in	grin	spin	inn	be-gin	cap-tain	dis-ci-pline
bin	kin	tin	jinn		cer-tain	fem-i-nine
chin	pin	thin	Quinn		vil-lain	mas-cu-line
din	shin	twin	Lynn	moc-ca-sin		gen-u-ine
fin	sin	win	Flynn	vi-o-lin		sac-char-ine
gin	skin	whin		jav-e-lin		
(1)	(2)	(3)	(4)	(5)	(6)	(7)

*See Family 198

Family 164

mince	since	rinse	blintze (*or* blintz)	nui-sance
prince	Vince			
quince	wince		chintz	
(1)	(2)	(3)	(4)	(5)

Family 165

(1)	(2)	(3)
inch	flinch	lynch
cinch	pinch	
clinch	squinch	
finch ☺	winch	

Family 166

(1)	(2)	(3)
binge	singe	sy-ringe
cringe	tinge	
fringe	twinge	
hinge		

*See Family 181

Family 167

(1)	(2)	(3)	(4)
dint	print	a-squint	pint
flint	splint	re-print	
glint	sprint	im-print	
hint	squint		
lint	stint		
mint	tint		

Family 168

(1)	(2)	(3)	(4)	(5)	(6)	☺
blip	grip	pip	sip	tip	gyp	grippe
chip	hip	quip	skip	trip		
clip	kip	rip	slip	whip		
dip	lip	scrip	snip	yip		
drip	nip	ship	strip	zip		
flip						

*See Family 200

Family 169

(1)	(2)	(3)
script	crypt	clipped
	Egypt	quipped

Family 170

(1)	(2)	(3)	(4)
bliss	this	a-miss	Be-a-trice
hiss		dis-miss	av-a-rice
kiss	Swiss	a-nal-y-sis	prej-u-dice
miss	priss		

*See Families 190 & 206

Family 171

(1)	(2)	(3)
dish fish swish wish	li-quor-ish (*adj. alcohol*)	lic-o-rice *n. also li-quo-rice* (candy)

Family 172

(1)	(2)
brisk disk (*or* disc) frisk risk whisk	bisque (*also* bisk)

Family 173

chrism
prism
schism
(1)

Family 174

crisp
lisp
wisp
(1)

Family 175

(1)	(2)	(3)	(4)
fist gist grist hist list mist	schist twist whist wist wrist	cyst tryst+	in-sist re-sist de-sist ex-ist

Family 176

bit	kit	slit	twit	ac-quit	com-mit	pred-i-cate
chit	knit	smit	whit	ad-mit	re-mit	pas-sion-ate
fit	lit	snit	wit	arm-pit	sub-mit	il-lit-er-ate
flit	pit	spit	writ	e-mit		
grit	quit	split			min-ute	fa-vor-ite
hit	sit	sprit	mitt			op-po-site
(1)	(2)	(3)	(4)	(5)	(6)	☺

*See Family 202

Family 177

itch	flitch	stitch	rich	niche
bitch	hitch	switch	which	
ditch	pitch	twitch		
fitch	snitch	witch ☺		
(1)	(2)	(3)	(4)	(5)

*See Families 28, 220, 249, 275, 331 & 338

Family 178

frith	myth	width
kith		
pith		
smith		
with		
(1)	(2)	(3)

Family 179

fix	pyx (*also* pix)	re-fix	knicks
mix	Styx		licks
nix			etc.
six			
(1)	(2)	(3)	(4)

Family 180

is	dizz	Liz
his	fizz	quiz
	frizz	whiz (*or* whizz)
	sizz	
(1)	(2)	(3)

ŋ

Family 181	bing	☺ king	sling	ring	
	bring	Ming	spring	wing	
	cling	ping	sting	wring	
	ding	ring	string	whing	
	fling	sing	swing	zing	
	(1)	(2)	(3)	(4)	

*See Family 166

Family 182	ink	dink	link	skink	zinc
	blink	drink	mink	slink	
	brink	fink	pink	stink	sync
	chink	jink	rink	tink	
	crink	kink	shrink	think	
		sink	wink		
	(1)	(2)	(3)	(4)	(5)

Family 183	tinct	pre-cinct	blinked
	dis-tinct	suc-cinct	linked
	ex-tinct	in-dis-tinct	winked
	(1)	(2)	(3)

Family 184	jinx	lynx
	minx	
	sphinx	
	(1)	(2)

ī

Family 185	by	my	sky	thy	a-wry
	cry	ply	sly	try	espy+
	dry	pry	spy	why	
	fly ☺	Sy	spry	wry	
	fry	shy	sty		
	(1)	(2)	(3)	(4)	(5)

Family 186

aye (*also* ay)	buy
bye	Guy
dye	
eye ☺	
lye	
rye	
(1)	(2)

Family 187

high	hi
nigh	
sigh	
thigh	
(1)	(2)

Family 188

die	pie
fie	tie
hie	vie
lie	
(1)	(2)

Family 189

bribe
gibe (*or jibe, to jeer*)
jibe (*also gibe, to agree; or gybe, a sail*)
scribe
tribe
(1)

*See Family 148

Family 190

ice	price	thrice	ad-vice	vise	gneiss
dice	rice	trice	de-vice		Par-a-dise
lice	slice	twice	suf-fice	ad-vise	
mice	spice	vice		ad-ver-tise	
nice			Weiss		
(1)	(2)	(3)	(4)	(5)	(6)

*See Families 170 & 206

Family 191

bide	pride	snide	guide	lied	con-fide
bride	ride	stride	mis-guide	spied	a-bide
chide	side	tide		tied	re-side
glide	slide	wide			col-lide
hide					
(1)	(2)	(3)	(4)	(5)	(6)

*See Family 151

Family 192

diet	riot	Wyatt
quiet		
dis-quiet		
(1)	(2)	(3)

Family 193

fife	rife
knife	strife
life	wife
(1)	(2)

*See Family 153

Family 194

bike ☹	Mike	tyke (*also* tike)	a-like
dike	pike		dis-like
hike	shrike		un-a-like
Ike	spike		
like	strike		
(1)	(2)	(3)	(4)

Family 195

bile	spile	dial	isle	guile	croc-o-dile
file	stile	trial	aisle	be-guile	ju-ve-nile
mile	tile	vial	lisle		
pile	vile				
rile	while	style			
smile	wile	chyle			
(1)	(2)	(3)	(4)	(5)	☺

Family 196	child mild	wild
	(1)	(2)

Family 197	clime chime crime dime grime	lime mime prime slime time	rhyme thyme chyme cyme	climb limn	sub-lime
	(1)	(2)	(3)	(4)	(5)

*See Family 161

Family 198

brine chine dine fine kine line mine	nine pine Rhine shine shrine sine spine	swine thine trine twine vine whine wine	stein	sign as-sign con-sign de-sign re-de-sign re-sign be-nign a-lign re-a-lign ma-lign en-sign	in-cline de-cline re-cline com-bine de-fine re-fine con-fine Al-pine su-pine o-pine	di-vine bo-vine ca-nine fe-line
(1)	(2)	(3)	(4)	(5)	(6)	(7)

*See Family 163

Family 199	bind blind find grind hind	kind mind rind wind	be-hind re-wind un-wind un-kind	un-bind pur-blind
	(1)	(2)	(3)	(4)

Family 200	gripe pipe ripe snipe stipe	stripe swipe tripe wipe yipe	hype type
*See Family 168	(1)	(2)	(3)

Family 201

ire	sire	byre	choir	a-fire	en-tire
dire	spire	gyre		ac-quire	re-tire
fire	squire	lyre	dryer	re-quire	as-pire
hire	tire	pyre	higher	in-quire	in-spire
mire	wire			es-quire	con-spire
shire		liar	buyer	at-tire	per-spire
(1)	(2)	(3)	(4)	(5)	☺

*See Families 132 & 351

Family 202

bite	smite	indict	incite	polite	height
cite	spite		excite	despite	sleight
kite	sprite		recite	finite	
mite	trite		contrite	requite	infinite
quite	white				
rite	write				
site					
(1)	(2)	(3)	(4)	(5)	(6)

*See Family 176

Family 203

bight	fright	right	a-light	fore-sight
blight	knight	sight	to-night	hind-sight
bright	light	slight	mid-night	play-wright
dight	might	tight	in-sight	
fight	night	wight		
flight	plight	wright		
(1)	(2)	(3)	(4)	(5)

Family 204

lithe	tithe	scythe
lithe	writhe	
(1)	(2)	(3)

Family 205

(1)	(2)	(3)	(4)	(5)	(6)
live (*adj.*)	rive	gyve	a-live	give	sieve
chive	shive		ar-rive	live (*verb*)	
dive	shrive		re-vive		
drive	strive		sur-vive		
five	thrive		con-nive		
hive	wive (*verb*)		en-dive		
jive			con-trive		

Family 206

(1)	(2)	(3)	(4)	(5)	(6)
rise	prize	guise	bap-tize	a-rise	un-wise
wise	size	dis-guise	crit-i-cize	ad-vise	tel-e-vise
			a-pol-o-gize	de-vise	im-pro-vise
			os-tra-cize	re-vise	oth-er-wise
				ap-prise	
				sur-prise	
				(*also* sur-prize)	

*See Families 170 & 190

AH or AW

Family 207

(1)	(2)	(3)
ah	bra	Baugh
bah	ba	
shah	ma	
	pa	
	spa	

Family 208

(1)	(2)	(3)	(4)	(5)	(6)
bob	gob	knob	sob	swab	daub+
blob	glob	lob	slob	squab	
cob	hob	mob	snob		
fob	job	rob	throb		shish-ke-bab

*See Family 248

Family 209

(1)	(2)	(3)	(4)	(5)	(☺)	(☺)
bock	crock	knock	sock	loch	boc	Bang-kok
block	dock	lock	shock	Bloch	hoc	
cock ☺	flock	mock	smock		roc	
chock	frock	pock	stock			
clock	hock	rock		Bach		

Family 210

(1)	(2)	(3)	(4)	(5)	(6)
cod	hod	pod	rod	odd	quad
clod	mod	plod	sod		squad
God	nod	prod	shod		wad
			scrod (*or* escrod)		
			trod		

*See Family 250

Family 211

(1)	(2)	(3)
dodge	hodge-podge	dis-lodge
hodge		
lodge		
podge		
stodge		

Family 212

(1)	(2)	(3)	(4)	(5)
bog	flog	log	a-gog	Prague
cog	frog	nog	de-fog	
clog	grog	slog	un-clog	
dog	hog	smog		
jog		tog		

Family 213

(1)	(2)	(3)	(4)	(5)
Dom	bomb	Guam	Viet Nam	a-plomb
mom				
pom				
prom				
Tom				

Family 214

(1)	(2)
alm(s)	psalm
balm	qualm
calm	em-balm
palm	

Family 215

(1)	(2)
clomp	swamp
pomp	
romp	
stomp	

Family 216

(1)	(2)	(3)	(4)	(5)	☺
on	yon	gone	wan	John	Yvonne
con	upon	be-gone	swan		
don	a-non	by-gone			Tucson

*See Family 317

Family 217

(1)	(2)	(3)	(4)	(5)	(6)
bop	drop	pop	slop	swap	a-top
cop	hop	plop	stop		es-top
clop	knop	prop	strop		
chop	lop	sop	top		
crop	mop	shop	whop		

*See Family 261

Family 218

(1)	(2)	(3)	(4)	(5)
bosh	posh	bosch	quash	ki-bosh
frosh	slosh		squash	ga-losh
gosh	splosh		wash	Mc-In-tosh
josh	tosh		swash	mac-in-tosh
nosh				

Family 219

(1)	(2)	(3)	(4)	(5)
blot	jot	sot	swat	watt
cot	knot	Scot	squat	
clot	lot	shot	a-squat	yacht
dot	al-lot	slot	kum-quat	
got	not	spot		
begot	plot	tot		
forgot	rot	trot		
not		a-pri-cot		

*Scc Family 264

Family 220

(1)	(2)	(3)
botch	notch	watch+
blotch	Scotch	swatch
crotch	splotch	
gotch		

*See Families 28, 177, 249, 275, 331 & 338

Family 221

(1)	(2)	(3)
broth	moth+	swath
Goth	sloth+	
cloth	troth+	
froth	wroth+	

*See Family 266

Family 222

(1)	(2)
ox	docks
box	socks
Cox	
fox	
Knox	

Family 223

(1)	(2)	(3)
ga-rage	en-tou-rage	mé-nage
bar-rage	cam-ou-flage	mi-rage
cor-sage	per-si-flage	
mas-sage	col-lage	

*See Families 41, 152

AW

Family 224

caw	haw	saw	awe	Ar-kan-sas
claw	jaw	slaw		
craw	law	squaw		O-ma-ha
draw	maw	straw		
flaw	paw	thaw		
gnaw	raw	yaw		
(1)	(2)	(3)	(4)	(5)

Family 225

fraud	broad
gaud	
laud	
Maud (*or* Maude)	
(1)	(2)

Family 226

off	cough	quaff
doff	trough	
scoff		
(1)	(2)	(3)

Family 227

oft	soft	coughed
croft	toft	soughed
loft	a-loft	
(1)	(2)	(3)

Family 228

awl	doll+	scrawl
bawl	loll+	shawl
brawl		sprawl
crawl		trawl
drawl		yawl
pawl (*also* pall *or* paul)		
pawl		
(1)	(2)	(3)

Family 229

all	mall	caul	ap-pall (*or* ap-pal)
ball	pall	Gaul	in-stall
call	small	haul	(*also* in-stal)
fall	squall	maul	
gall	squall (*or* squawl)	Paul	
hall	tall	Saul	
	wall		
(1)	(2)	(3)	(4)

Family 230

auld	bald
	scald
(1)	(2)

Family 231

balk	stalk	gawk	auk
calk (*or* caulk, a cleat)	talk	hawk ☺	
chalk	walk	squawk	
(1)	(2)	(3)	(4)

Family 232

halt	fault
alt	vault
salt	
(1)	(2)

Family 233

Schmaltz
waltz
(1)

Family 234

solve	e-volve
dis-solve	in-volve
(1)	(2)

Family 235

awn	lawn	faun	Sean
brawn	pawn		
dawn	sawn		
drawn	yawn		
fawn ☺			
(1)	(2)	(3)	(4)

*See Families 269 & 280

Family 236

(1)
craunch
haunch
launch
paunch
staunch

Family 237

(1)	(2)	(3)	(4)
aunt+	haunt	want	font
daunt	jaunt		
flaunt	taunt		
gaunt	vaunt		

Family 238

(1)	(2)	(3)
bond	wand	be-yond
blond (*or* blonde)		re-spond
fond		cor-re-spond
frond		
pond		

Family 239

(1)	(2)	(3)	(4)
bong	gong	song	a-long
Cong	long	strong	be-long
dong	pong	throng	pro-long
flong	prong	wrong	

Family 240

(1)	
conk	conch
clonk	
honk	

Family 241

(1)	(2)	(3)	(4)
boss	loss	haus	a-cross
cross	moss	em-boss	
dross	toss		
gloss	fosse (*or* foss)	saùce	la crosse

Family 242			
	cost frost lost	un-lost	bossed crossed etc.
	(1)	(2)	(3)

Family 243				
	aught caught fraught naught taught	bought brought fought nought	ought sought thought wrought	taut
	(1)	(2)	(3)	(4)

Family 244				
	cause clause pause	ap-plause be-cause	gauze hawse	Santa Claus
	(1)	(2)	(3)	(4)

Family 245					
	doe foe floe hoe Joe Poe	roe sloe schmoe toe throe woe	ap-ro-pos	po-ta-to to-ma-to	al-to pi-an-o so-pra-no sew
	(1)	(2)	(3)	(4)	(5)

Family 246

Bo go Flo fro oh!	ho lo no so	though dough al-though thor-ough	owe Lowe Rowe	beau tab-leau bu-reau pla-teau Mar-geaux Bor-deaux	de-pot Mar-got sa-bot ja-bot mot	a-go ban-jo buf-fa-lo er-go Mex-i-co
(1)	(2)	(3)	(4)	(5)	(6)	☺

Family 247

bow	grow	show	in-flow	a-glow	a-row
blow	know	slow	out-flow	be-low	ar-row
Crow	low	snow	over-flow	bun-ga-low	el-bow
crow ☺	mow	stow	over-grow	be-stow	bor-row
flow	row	tow	over-throw	es-crow	sor-row
glow	sow	throw			to-mor-row
(1)	(2)	(3)	(4)	(5)	☺

*See Family 271

Family 248

globe	strobe	Job
lobe	robe	Mich-e-lob
probe	dis-robe	
(1)	(2)	(3)

*See Family 208

Family 249

broach	brooch	ap-proach
coach		re-proach
loach		en-croach
poach		cock-roach
roach		
(1)	(2)	(3)

*See Families 28, 177, 220, 275, 331, & 338

Family 250

ode	abode	goad	hoed
bode	a-la-mode	load	toed
code	com-mode	road	etc.
mode	cor-rode	toad ☺	owed
rode	dis-com-mode		blowed
strode			
(1)	(2)		(4)

*See Family 210

Family 251

brogue	col-logue
Hogue	pi-rogue
rogue	pro-rogue
togue	
vogue	
(1)	(2)

Family 252

(1)	(2)	(3)	(4)	(5)
bloke	sloke	woke	a-woke	con-voke
coke	☺ smoke	yoke	pro-voke	
choke	spoke	re-voke	ar-ti-choke	
joke	stoke	e-voke	be-spoke	
poke	stroke			

Family 253

(1)	(2)	(3)
oak	folk	toque
soak	yolk	
coak		eq-ui-voque
cloak		
croak		

Family 254

(1)	(2)	(3)	(4)	(5)
boll	scroll	bowl	a-toll	sol
droll	stroll	jowl+	en-roll	ex-tol (*also* extoll)
knoll	troll		(*or* enrol)	pa-trol
roll	toll			con-trol
poll				

Family 255

(1)	(2)	(3)
coal	goal	char-coal
foal	shoal	

Family 256

(1)	(2)	(3)	(4)
bole	role	pa-role	soul
cole	sole	in-sole	
dole	stole	re-sole	
hole	thole	con-sole	
mole	whole	ca-jole	
pole		cas-ser-ole	

Family 257

bold	old	un-fold	un-told
cold	sold	en-hold	re-told
fold	scold	in-fold	re-sold
gold	told	be-hold	Le-o-pold
hold	wold	up-hold	man-i-fold
mold (*or* mould)			mar-i-gold
			mul-ti-fold
(1)	(2)	(3)	(4)

Family 258

bolt	jolt	re-volt	poult	a-dult
colt	molt (*or* moult)		in-sult	
dolt	smolt		re-sult	
holt	volt		con-sult	
			ex-ult	
(1)	(2)	(3)	(4)	(5)

Family 259

brome	Nome	foam	ohm	comb
chrome	pome	loam		cat-a-comb
dome	Rome	roam	poem+	
gnome	tome			
home	Je-rome			
(1)	(2)	(3)	(4)	(5)

Family 260

bone	hone	shone	a-lone	cy-clone	Co-logne
cone	lone	stone	a-tone	trom-bone	
clone	prone	tone	de-throne	sax-o-phone	
crone	phone	throne		bar-i-tone	
drone	Rhone	zone			
(1)	(2)	(3)	(4)	(5)	(6)

Family 261

(1)	(2)	(3)	(4)	(5)
cope	lope	slope	e-lope	can-ta-loupe
dope	mope	scope	en-ve-lope	(*also* cantaloup)
grope	pope		mis-an-thrope	(*or* cantalope)
hope	rope	taupe	an-te-lope	(*or* cantelope)
		soap	tel-e-scope	

*See Family 217

Family 262

(1)	(2)	(3)	(4)
close (*adv.*)	gross	jo-cose	di-ag-nose
dose	en-gross	mo-rose	bel-li-cose
		glu-cose	co-ma-tose
		over-dose	cel-lu-lose
		ver-bose	gran-di-ose
			ad-i-pose

*See Family 268

Family 263

(1)	(2)	(3)	(4)
oast	host	ri-poste (*also* ripost)	ut-most
boast	☺ ghost		fore-most
coast	most		upper-most
roast	post		further-most
toast			

Family 264

(1)	(2)	(3)	(4)
dote	smote	e-mote	de-note
mote	tote	re-mote	con-note
note	vote	pro-mote	an-ec-dote
rote	wrote	de-vote	an-ti-dote

*See Family 219

Family 265

oat	goat ☺
boat	moat
bloat	throat
coat	a-float
float	
gloat	
(1)	(2)

Family 266

both	growth	loathe (*v.*)	oath	be-troth+
sloth+		loath+		be-he-moth+
wroth+		(*or* loth		
troth+		*also* loathe, *adj.*)		
(1)	(2)	(3)	(4)	(5)

*See Family 221

Family 267

cove	hove	strove	mauve+	al-cove
clove	Jove	trove		man-grove
dove	rove	throve		
drove	shrove	wove		
grove	stove			
(1)	(2)	(3)	(3)	(4)

*See Families 309 & 356

Family 268

chose	doze	a-rose	im-pose
close	froze	en-close	com-pose
hose	gloze	dis-close	pro-pose
nose		de-pose	sup-pose
pose	beaux	dis-pose	op-pose
prose	(*or* beaus)	ex-pose	inter-pose
rose ☺		re-pose	
(1)	(2)	(3)	(4)

*See Family 262

Family 269	own	sown	groan	sewn
	blown	shown	loan	
	flown	thrown	moan	
	grown	dis-own	roan	
	known	un-known	be-moan	
	mown		Joan	
	(1)	(2)	(3)	(4)

*See Families 235 & 280

Family 270	
	coax
	hoax
	(1)

OU

Family 271

	bow	now	bough	thou	a-vow
	brow	plow (*or* plough)	plough		dis-a-vow
☺	cow	row	slough+		al-low
	chow	sow			dis-al-low
	frow	scow			en-dow
	how	vow			bow-wow
	mow	wow			pow-wow
	(1)	(2)	(3)	(4)	(5)

*See Family 247

Family 272	owl ☺	growl	prowl	foul
	cowl	howl	scowl	be-foul
	fowl	jowl		
	(1)	(2)	(3)	(4)

Family 273

bowel	towel	a-vowal	dis-em-bowel
dowel	trowel	dis-a-vowal	
rowel	vowel		
(1)	(2)	(3)	(4)

Family 274

Al	Hal	shall	mo-rale	La-Salle	cor-ral
Cal	pal				bac-cha-nal
gal					
(1)	(2)	(3)	(4)	(5)	(6)

Family 275

ouch	pouch
couch	slouch
crouch	vouch
grouch	a-vouch
(1)	(2)

Family 276

cloud	crowd	a-loud
loud		be-cloud
proud		en-shroud
shroud		
(1)	(2)	(3)

Family 277

ounce	pounce	de-nounce	counts
bounce	rounce	re-nounce	a-mounts
flounce	trounce	pro-nounce	
	an-nounce		
(1)	(2)	(3)	(4)

Family 278

ground	pound	a-bound	pro-found	un-sound
found	round	re-bound	con-found	re-sound
ground	sound	un-bound	dum-found	re-dound
hound	wound	in-bound	ex-pound	a-stound
mound		out-bound	im-pound	sur-round
		a-round	pro-pound	a-ground
(1)	(2)	(3)	(4)	(5)

Family 279

(1)	(2)	(3)
count	a-mount	ac-count
fount	dis-mount	re-count
mount	sur-mount	dis-count
	par-a-mount	tan-ta-mount

Family 280

(1)	(2)	(3)	(4)	(5)
brown	down	gown	noun	own
clown	drown	town	pro-noun	
crown	frown	re-nown		

*See Families 235 & 269

Family 281

(1)	(2)	(3)	(4)	(5)	(6)
blouse	house	souse	Kraus	Grauss	nous+
chouse	louse	spouse			
grouse	mouse	es-pouse			

Family 282

(1)	(2)	(3)
oust	Faust	doused
joust		housed+
roust		soused

Family 283

(1)	(2)	(3)	(4)	(5)	☺
out	grout	scout	stout	doubt	drought+
bout	knout	shout	tout		(*or* drouth)
clout	lout	spout	trout	a-bout	
flout	pout	sprout		de-vout	
gout	rout	snout	route+	kraut	

Family 284

(1)	(2)	(3)
drought+ (*or* drouth)	Fal-mouth	ver-mouth
Louth	Ply-mouth	
mouth		
south		

Family 285

(1)	(2)	(3)	(4)	(5)	(6)
bower	lower (*or* lour)	em-power	our	hour	de-vour
cower	power		dour	sour	
flower	shower		flour	scour	

*See Family 352

Family 286

(1)	(2)	(3)	(4)
browse (*or* browze)	blouse	rouse+(*v.*)	a-rouse
drowse	douse	touse+	ca-rouse
touse (*or* towse)	house (*v.*)		es-pouse+

ŌR̃

Family 287

(1)	(2)	(3)	(4)	(5)	(6)
or	oar	door	four	war	ab-hor
for	boar	floor	pour	corps	cred-i-tor
nor	roar				gov-er-nor
Thor	soar				Cor-reg-i-dor
		di-no-saur			pos-te-ri-or

Family 288

(1)	(2)	(3)	(4)	(5)
bore	more	snore	ex-plore	ga-lore
core	ore	store	im-plore	a-shore
chore	pore	swore	de-plore	re-store
fore	sore	tore	en-core	syc-a-more
frore	score	wore	ig-nore	soph-o-more
gore	shore	yore	a-dore	The-o-dore
lore			be-fore	

Family 289

bord (*also* board)	ac-cord	board	ward
cord	re-cord (*v.*)	a-board	a-ward
chord	rec-ord	hoard	re-ward
ford	af-ford	for-ward	
fjord (*or* fiord)	harp-si-chord		
Lord			
sword	horde	gourd	
(1)	(2)	(3)	(4)

Family 290

cork	torque	re-cork
fork		un-cork
pork		
stork ☺		
York		
(1)	(2)	(3)

Family 291

form	warm	in-form	mis-in-form
dorm	swarm	re-form	per-form
norm		de-form	u-ni-form
storm			
(1)	(2)	(3)	(4)

Family 292

born	shorn	warn	borne	mourn	a-corn
corn	sworn		for-borne	be-mourn	a-dorn
horn	torn				for-sworn
lorn	thorn				u-ni-corn
morn	worn				Cap-ri-corn
					for-lorn
(1)	(2)	(3)	(4)	(5)	(6)

Family 293

gorse	coarse	course	source	di-vorce
horse	hoarse	re-course	re-source	en-force
Morse		con-course	re-in-force	en-dorse
		dis-course		
(1)	(2)	(3)	(4)	(5)

Family 294

bort	sport	court	wart	air-port	con-sort
fort	snort		thwart	re-port	a-bort
port	tort		quart	com-port	ca-vort
short	wort			con-tort	es-cort
				dis-tort	sup-port
(1)	(2)	(3)	(4)	(5)	(6)

Family 295

forth	fourth	swarth
north		
(1)	(2)	(3)

OI

Family 296

boy	ploy	a-hoy	en-joy	buoy+	Ha-noi
coy	Roy	al-loy	con-voy		
cloy	soy	de-ploy	an-noy	St. Croix	Il-li-nois
joy	toy	em-ploy	en-voy		
(1)	(2)	(3)	(4)	(5)	(6)

Family 297

choice	Joyce
voice	
re-joice	
in-voice	
(1)	(2)

Family 298

oil	moil	re-coil	loyal	Hoyle
boil	soil	em-broil	royal	gar-goyle
broil	toil	tur-moil		
roil	spoil			
coil			voile	
foil				
(1)	(2)	(3)	(4)	(5)

Family 299

(1)	(2)	(3)
coin	ad-join	Des Moines
groin	con-join	
join	re-join	
loin		
quoin		

Family 300

(1)	(2)	(3)
noise	counter-poise	toys
poise	tur-quoise	boys

Family 301

(1)	(2)
hoist	voiced
foist	re-joiced
joist	
moist	

a

Family 302

(1)	(2)	(3)
blub	hub	snub
cub	nub	slub
club	pub	stub
chub	rub	scrub
dub	sub	shrub
drub	tub	
flub		

*See Family 337

Family 303

(1)	(2)	(3)	(4)	(5)
buck	muck	shuck	amok	wood-chuck
chuck	puck	stuck	(*or* amuck)	Ca-nuck
cluck	pluck	struck		awe-struck
duck ☺	ruck	tuck		saw-buck
luck	suck	truck		

Family 304

(1)	(2)
duct	pro-duct
ab-duct	a-que-duct
in-duct	con-struct
con-duct	in-struct
mis-con-duct	ob-struct
de-duct	vi-a-duct

Family 305

(1)	(2)	(3)
bud	sud	blood
Bud	scud	flood
crud	spud	
cud	stud	
dud	thud	
mud		

*See Family 340

Family 306

(1)	(2)	(3)	(4)
budge	grudge	sludge	ad-judge
drudge	judge	smudge	pre-judge
fudge	nudge	trudge	be-grudge

Family 307

(1)	(2)	(3)	(4)
buff	fluff	ruff	chough
bluff	guff	scuff	clough+
cuff	gruff	snuff	rough
chuff	huff	stuff	sough+
duff	muff	scruff	slough+
	puff	re-buff	e-nough

Family 308

(1)	(2)	(3)
bug ☺	mug	snug
dug	pug	shrug
drug	plug	chug
fug	rug	tug
hug	slug	thug
jug	smug	un-plug
lug		

*See Family 342

Family 309	love	shove	of
	glove	a-bove	where-of
	dove		there-of
	(1)	(2)	(3)

*See Families 267 & 356

Family 310	cull	lull	skull	an-nul
	dull	mull	stull	
	gull ☺	null	trull	
	hull	scull		
	(1)	(2)	(3)	(4)

Family 311	bulk	sulk
	hulk	skulk (*also* sculk)
	(1)	(2)

Family 312	gulp
	pulp
	sculp
	(1)

Family 313

bum	mum	stum	au-tumn	sor-ghum
chum	plum	scrum	col-umn	
drum	rum	strum		
gum	sum	swum		
glum	scum	thrum		
hum	slum	tum		
(1)	(2)	(3)	(4)	(5)

*See Family 346

Family 314	crumb	come	Mal-colm
	dumb	some	
	numb	be-come	
	plumb	tire-some	
	thumb		
	rhumb		
	suc-cumb		
	(1)	(2)	(3)

Family 315

bump	frump	mump(s)	sump	thump
chump	grump	pump	slump	thrump
clump	hump	plump	stump	trump
crump	jump	rump	tump	ump
dump	lump			
(1)	(2)	(3)	(4)	(5)

Family 316

bun	nun	stun	be-gun	ac-tion	fis-sion
dun	pun	sun	over-run	na-tion	mis-sion
fun	run	tun	out-run		
gun	shun				
Hun	spun				
(1)	(2)	(3)	(4)	(5)	(6)

*See Family 347

Family 317

one (**1**)	hon	out-done	ac-tion	A-sian	as-cen-sion
done	mon	over-done	na-tion	Eu-ra-sian	de-clen-sion
none	ton				
	son				
	won				
	re-won				
(1)	(2)	(3)	(4)	(5)	(6)

*See Family 216

Family 318

once	dunce
(1)	(2)

Family 319

bunch	munch
brunch	punch
crunch	scrunch
hunch	
lunch	
(1)	(2)

Family 320

bund	or-o-tund
fund	ob-ro-tund
ob-tund	ro-tund
re-fund	ru-bi-cund
mor-i-bund	cum-mer-bund
(1)	(2)

Family 321

bung	lung	stung	tongue	young
clung	rung	sung		
dung	slung	swung		
flung	sprung	wrung		
hung	strung	un-strung		
(1)	(2)	(3)	(4)	(5)

Family 322

blunge	ex-punge	sponge
lunge	mus-kel-lunge	
plunge		
(1)	(2)	(3)

Family 323

bunk	flunk	skunk	de-bunk	monk
chunk	gunk	slunk		
clunk	hunk	spunk		
dunk	junk	shrunk		
drunk	punk	trunk		
funk	plunk			
sunk				
(1)	(2)	(3)	(4)	(5)

Family 324

bunt	grunt	runt	front
blunt	hunt	shunt	wont
brunt	punt ☺	stunt	af-front
			con-front
(1)	(2)	(3)	(4)

Family 325			
	up	7-Up	de-vel-op (*also* de-vel-ope)
	cup	hic-cup	
	gup		
	pup		
	scup		
	(1)	(2)	(3)

Family 326				
us	buss	am-o-rous	out-ra-geous	e-gre-gious
bus	cuss	dan-ger-ous	ad-van-ta-geous	con-ta-gious
Gus	fuss	fu-ri-ous		
pus	muss	se-ri-ous		por-poise
plus	truss	ca-lam-i-tous		
rhus	dis-cuss			
thus				
(1)	(2)	(3)	(4)	(5)

Family 327				
	blush	hush	slush	push
	brush	lush	tush	bush
	crush	mush+	thrush	
	flush	plush		
	gush	rush		
	(1)	(2)	(3)	(4)

Family 328			
	busk	musk	brusque (*also* brusk)
	cusk	rusk	
	dusk	tusk	
	husk		
	(1)	(2)	(3)

Family 329				
bust	lust	ad-just	dis-gust	re-ad-just
crust	must	un-just	mis-trust	
dust	rust	dis-trust	ro-bust	
gust	trust	Au-gust	en-trust	
just	thrust			
(1)	(2)	(3)	(4)	(5)

Family 330

but	hut	scut	strut	butt	what	co-co-nut
cut	jut	shut	tut	mutt		pea-nut
gut	nut	slut	a-but	(*also* mut)	put	hal-i-but
glut	rut	smut	re-but	putt		
(1)	(2)	(3)	(4)	(5)	(6)	☺

*See Family 350

Family 331

cutch	Dutch	much	touch
clutch	hutch	such	re-touch
crutch	smutch		
(1)	(2)	(3)	(4)

*See Families 28, 177, 220, 249, 275, 338

Family 332

crux
flux
in-flux
(1)

Family 333

buzz	coz	does	was	huz	'cause+
fuzz			'twas		because+
a-buzz					
(1)	(2)	(3)	(4)	(5)	(6)

U or OO

Family 334

OO			U				
blew	drew	screw	few	phew	Hugh	a-skew	view
brew	flew	shrew	hew	skew	Pugh	neph-ew	
chew	grew	stew	mew(s)	slew		cur-few	
crew	grew	strew	pew	spew		cash-ew	
dew	knew	new		smew	ewe		
(1)	(2)	(3)	(4)	(5)	(6)	☺	☺

Family 335

OO			U			
blue	Con-fu	Sioux	An-jou	ra-gout	cue	ar-gue
clue	E-li-hu		Ca-chou	sur-tout	due	en-sue
glue	Hin-du	pooh	Man-i-tou		hue	
rue	Zu-lu				im-bue	
Sue	fi-chu	de-but			pre-vue	
slue	Ku-Ku				bar-be-cue	
true		slough+	queue		av-e-nue	
(1)	(2)	(3)	(4)	(5)	(6)	(7)

Family 336

U	OO				
you	boo	do	shoe	bal-ly-hoo	hul-loo
bay-ou	coo	to	ca-noe	bam-boo	hoo-doo
	goo	who		boo-boo	ig-loo
lieu	moo		two	tat-too	voo-doo
a-dieu	too	a-do		boo-hoo	☺ kan-ga-roo
	woo	out-do		cock-a-too	koo-doo
	zoo	over-do		ta-boo	ya-hoo
		to-do		cuck-oo	peek-a-boo
		un-do		sham-poo	yoo-hoo
		re-do		goo-goo	
(1)	(2)	(3)	(4)	(5)	(6)

Family 337

U	OO	U *or* OO
cube	boob	in-ner-tube
tube		
lube		
(1)	(2)	(3)

*See Family 302

Family 338

hooch	pooch
mooch	smooch
(1)	(2)

*See Families 28, 177, 220, 249, 275 & 331

Family 339	brood food mood	rood snood	pre-lude
	(1)	(2)	(3)

*See Family 358

Family 340

crude dude nude prude rude	lewd shrewd	screwed stewed strewed	Ger-trude in-trude ex-ude pro-trude ap-ti-tude at-ti-tude	be-at-i-tude for-ti-tude lat-i-tude lon-gi-tude in-ter-lude pul-chri-tude	feud
(1)	(2)	(3)	(4)	(5)	(6)

*See Family 305

Family 341	goof hoof+ proof roof woof	dis-proof a-loof
	(1)	(2)

Family 342

	OO		U	
	stooge Scrooge	rouge+	huge ref-uge	del-uge sub-ter-fuge
	(1)	(2)	(3)	(4)

*See Family 308

Family 343

	OO		U
Fa-rouk	duke fluke ☺ juke nuke pe-ruke	gook+ kook snook+ spook	puke re-buke Du-buque
(1)	(2)	(3)	(4)

*See Family 359

Family 344

U			OO		
mule	duel+	mewl	rule	dual	gruel
pule	fuel				cruel
yule		you'll	who'll	ghoul	
	jewel				
(1)	(2)	(3)	(4)	(5)	(6)

Family 345

cool	school	re-tool
drool	spool	
fool	stool	
pool	tool	
(1)	(2)	(3)

Family 346

OO					U
flume	re-sume	bloom	groom	tomb	fume
plume	con-sume	boom	loom	womb	spume
as-sume	sub-sume	broom	room	en-tomb	per-fume
pre-sume	ex-hume	doom	zoom	bomb	
cos-tume		gloom			
re-sume					
	Khar-toum		rheum		
(1)	(2)	(3)	(4)	(5)	☺

*See Family 313

Family 347

OO					U
boon	moon	buf-foon	dune	at-tune	for-tune+
coon	noon	ba-boon	June	je-june	com-mune
croon	soon	sa-loon	prune		Nep-tune
goon	spoon	car-toon	tune	strewn	
loon	swoon	rac-coon			im-pugn
		(ra-coon,*also*)			
		ma-roon (*v.*)			hewn
		ma-roon (*n.*)			
		(*or* mar-roon)			
		bas-soon			
(1)	(2)	(3)	(4)	(5)	(6)

*See Family 316

Family 348

		ruin bruin	Rouen	doin'
		(1)	(2)	(3)

Family 349

coop	scoop	croup	dupe	coupe	re-group
droop	sloop	group	stupe	troupe	re-coup
goop	snoop	soup			
hoop	stoop	stoup			
loop	troop				
poop	whoop				
(1)	(2)	(3)	(4)	(5)	(6)

Family 350

OO				U		
boot	scoot	bruit	lute	jute	re-fute	foot
coot	shoot	fruit	brute	mute	con-fute	soot
hoot	toot	suit	chute		im-pute	
loot	ga-loot	re-cruit	flute		dis-pute	Butte
moot	ca-hoot(s)	cir-cuit			a-cute	
root			as-tute		com-mute	newt
	route+		dis-so-lute			
			res-o-lute			
(1)	(2)	(3)	(4)	(5)	☺	(7)

*See Family 330

Family 351

U			R̃	OO	
cure	you're	en-dure	sure	newer	lure
pure		ma-nure	un-sure	sewer	al-lure
	a-zure	ma-ture+	sure+		pro-cure
		in-ure	as-sure		
	Fuhrer+		un-sure		
	furor+	fewer	sig-na-ture		
		skewer	min-i-a-ture		
(1)	(2)	(3)	(4)	(5)	(6)

*See Families 132 & 201

Family 352

(1)	(2)	(3)
tour	a-mour	boor
your	de-tour	Moor
	con-tour	moor
	par-a-mour	poor
		spoor

*See Family 285

Family 353

OO				U		
goose	Bruce	sluice	mousse	juice	use	*(noun)*
loose	spruce				a-buse	"
moose	truce	nous	deuce	puce	dis-use	"
noose					mis-use	"
un-loose			re-fuse (*v.*)		ref-use	"
(1)	(2)	(3)	(4)	(5)	(6)	

Family 354

(1)	(2)	(3)	(4)
boost	loosed	juiced	Proust+
roost			

Family 355

th				th	
ruth	couth	booth	sleuth	smooth	soothe
truth	youth	sooth			
		tooth			
(1)	(2)	(3)	(4)	(5)	(6)

Family 356

(1)	(2)	(3)	(4)	(5)
move	im-prove	dis-ap-prove	groove	Louvre
prove	dis-prove	re-prove		
	ap-prove			

*See Families 267 & 309

Family 357

OO						U
booze	choose	bruise	lose	use(*v.*)	re-use(*v.*)	mews
ooze		cruise	whose	fuse	a-buse(*v.*)	news
snooze				muse	dif-fuse	
	do's			ruse	con-fuse	dues
(1)	(2)	(3)	(4)	(5)	(6)	☺

Family 358

could	good	live-li-hood	fool-har-di-hood
should	hood	like-li-hood	
would	stood	false-hood	
	wood	mis-un-der-stood	
(1)	(2)	(3)	(4)

*See Family 339

Family 359

book	nook	be-took	snook+
brook	rook	for-sook	spook
cook	shook	mis-took	
crook	schnook		
hook	took		
look			
(1)	(2)	(3)	(4)

*See Family 343

Family 360

bull ☺	wool	aw-ful	a-ble	can-cel
full		law-ful	ta-ble	
pull	me-dal			
	pe-dal			
(1)	(2)	(3)	(4)	(5)

Family 361

bush
push
cush
(1)

GREAT

DERIVATIVES

Ă

D 1

tax-i-cab	cabby (*or* cabbie)	hab-it	
fab-u-lous	gabby		
lab-o-ra-tory	flabby	rab-bit	dabs
1	2	3	4

D 2

yak-ked	back-er	pack-age	brack-ish	shel-lac
	crack-er			(& shel-lack)
lack-ed				
pack-ed		Jack-o'lantern		
		(& Jack-a-lantern)	rack-et	lac-quer
			(& rac-quet)	(& lack-er)
	kha-ki			biv-ouac
1	2	3	♥	5

D 3

action	actor	acts
traction	tractor	facts
1	2	3

D 4

caddie	gladly	madder	saddest	grad-u-ate	pads
(*or* caddy)	sadly	sadder	gladdest	grad-u-al	adding
1	2	3	4	♥	6

DERIVATIVES

D 5

1	2
ad-age	gad-get

D 6

1	2	3	4
pho-to-graph par-a-graph	sap-phire	laugh-ter daugh-ter	riff-raff

D 7

1	2	3	4
after rafter	crafty	witch-craft	rafts crafts

D 8

1	2	3	4	5	♥
braggart baggage	gagging wagging	haggard laggard	zig-zag	bags	dagger

D 9

1	2	3	4
glamour (*or* glamor) clamor	ramming cramming	dam-age salm-on (*silent l*)	hams jams

D 10

1	2	3	4
champ cham-pi-on-ship	damper camper	rampage	tram-po-line

D 11

1	2	3	4	5
me-chan-ic canon cannon canyon	Francis	man-a-ger hand-some plan-e-tar-i-um	bandy candy brandy	banner manner tanner

D 12	dancing ♥ chancing 1	ad-vance-ment 2	dances chances 3			
D 13	branches 1	ranches 2				
D 14	ban-dage 1	gran-di-ose bands hands 2	gran-deur brandish 3	blandish 4	hand-i-ly 5	
D 15	Bangor clangor 1	hanger 2	hangar 3	gangster 4	boo-mer-ang ♥	bangs gangs ♥
D 16	canker banker hanker hand-ker-chief (*silent d*) 1	ankle Frank-en-stein prank-ster 2	Yankee ranks 3	swanky 4	banks ♥	
D 17	ant-lers 1	pan-ther 2	canter planter 3	grant-or 4	grants pants 5	
D 18	cap-i-tal cap-i-tol 1	mapping napping 2	chap-lain 3	caps maps 4	re-cap-ture cap-ture 5	

DERIVATIVES

D 21

1	2	3	4	5
sarsaparilla (*silent r*)	em-bar-rass ha-rass+	classes glasses	pastime	raspberry (*silent p*)

D 22

1	2	3	4	♥
ashes	flashes	rashes	pass-ion	fash-ion

D 23

1	2
asks	tasks

D 25

1	2
gasps	clasps

D 26

1	2	3
e-las-tic fan-tas-tic	plaster	casts masts

D 27

1	2	3	4	♥	♥	7
battle cattle rattle	batted chatted matted	batter fatter matter	flattest fattest	cattiest rattiest nattiest	catty fatty natty	cattily nattily

D 28

1	2
catches matches latches	bach-e-lor

D 29

1	2	3
math-e-mat-ics	baths	paths

D 30	gavel gravel 1	calves (*also* calfs) 2
D 31	axes taxes 1	backs tacks 2
D 32	asthma (*silent th*) 1	

Ā

D 33	bays prays 1	has-ten (*silent t*) 2	baby 3		
D 34	cro-chet-ed ric-o-chet-ed (*or* ricochetted) 1	treys preys 2	fil-lets cro-chets 3		
D 35	pince-nez (*pans-na*) 1	neighs weighs 2	leis 3	mat-i-nees soi-rees 4	se-ance ♥
D 36	facing gracing lacing 1	aces faces 2			

DERIVATIVES

D 37

e-ra-sing 1

D 38

fading grading trading 1

D 39

aiding braiding 1	aids maids 2

D 40

chafing strafing 1	chafes strafes 2	chafe 3	waif 4

D 41

aging paging caging 1

D 42

aching 1	baking faking 2	baker maker 3

D 43

sca-ling 1	paler staler 2	azalea 3

D 44	sailor tailor jailor (*or* jailer) 1	nails ails 2	daily 3		
D 45	fa-mous in-fa-mous 1	blamable 2	blaming naming 3	a-mi-a-ble 4	
D 46	claim-ant 1	aims claims 2	ex-cla-ma-tion 3		
D 47	craning waning 1	san-i-ty van-i-ty 2			
D 48	main-tain sus-tain 1	gaining raining 2	gains pains 3	bar-gain 4	main-ten-ance 5
D 49	reins veins 1	reining 2	reign-ing feign-ing 3	deigns feigns 4	
D 50	ranging changing 1	change-a-ble 2			

DERIVATIVES

D 51	painting tainting 1		paints saints 2	
D 52	aping draping scraping 1		cap-a-ble shap-a-ble (*or* shapeable) 2	
D 53	basting pasting 1			bastes pastes 2
D 54	ir-ri-ta-ble tol-er-a-ble 1	dated fated 2	rating skating 3	un-grate-ful in-fla-ted 4
D 55	straits 1			waits 2
D 56		bathing scathing 1		
D 57	bravery knavery 1		pavement cav-i-ty 2	raving shaving 3
D 58	blazing gazing hazing 1	a-maz-ing 2	a-maze-ment 3	razor 4

D 59	raising praising 1	braised 2	phased 3	

AR

D 60	rep-er-toire memoir	bor-row	barring jarring	marred parred
	bar-room 1	bi-zarre (& bazar) 2	ba-zaar 3	hearth 4
D 61	Darby 1	Barbie 2	barbs 3	
D 62	arching marching 1			arches marches 2
D 63	carded larded 1	guarded 2	cards yards 3	guards 4
D 64	barfing scarfing 1	scarves (*or* scarfs) 2	wharves (*also* wharfs) 3	
D 65	ser-geant 1	barging charging 2	charge-able 3	

D 66

1	2	3	4
darken	carking barking	marked parked	parks sharks

D 67

1	2	3
snarling	gnarls snarls	quar-reled (*or* quar-relled *or* quarled)

D 68

1	2
arming charming	farms harms

D 69

1	2
darning	darns yarns

D 70

1	2	3
carping harping	sharpening	carps harps

D 72

1	2
carted parted smarted	carts parts

ĀR̃

D 74

1
daring caring

D 75

tearing	erring	error	bearer	heir-ess
wearing	terror			
	bar-ren	heron		
	bar-rel		nar-row	
1	2	3	4	♥

D 76

dairy	airing	stairway	fairs	ne'er-do-well	prai-rie
repairing			chairs	aer-o-sol	
1	2	3	4	5	6

Ĕ

D 77

ebbing	webbing	webs
		rebs
1	2	3

D 78

wrecked	trekked	decks	reckon	Czech-o-slo-va-ki-a
checked		flecks	beckon	
	break-fast			dis-co-theque
1	2	3	4	♥

D 79

sec-tion	de-tec-tive	ar-chi-tec-ture
in-ter-sec-tion	ob-jec-tive	
con-nec-tion	pro-tec-tive	
1	2	3

D 80

bedding	spreading	beds	in-cred-u-lous
wedding	dreading	shreds	in-cred-i-ble
1	2	3	4

DERIVATIVES

D 81	edging hedging hedging knowl-edge-able	fledg-ling fledged	ac-knowl-edg-ment (*also* acknowledgement)	ed-u-ca-tion
	1	2	3	4

D 82	deft-ness (*silent t*)	deafness	referee	hefty heif-er	clefts thefts	chefs refs
	1	2	3	4	♥	♥

D 83	begged pegged	begs	eggs	beggar
	1	2	3	4

D 84	jealousy	impelled repelled expelled	jells sells	wel-come	wel-fare
	1	2	3	4	♥

D 85	belches squelches	selfless	selfish shellfish	helping yelping shelves	elves (*also* elfs) selves
	1	2	3	4	5

D 86	smelter welter	delta	melting pelting
	1	2	3

D 87	healthy stealthy	wealth-i-er	delving shelving	twelfths
	1	2	3	4

D 88

1	2
hemming	stems
stemming	hems

D 89

1	2
tempting	tempts
at-tempting	

D 90

1	2	3	♥	♥
comedienne (*female*)	women	penning	hens	many
Wednesday		pens		
		ven-geance		

D 91

1	2	3
de-fen-si-ble	dis-pen-sa-ble	sensing
sen-si-ble		tensing

D 92

1	2
clenching	benches
quenching	drenches

D 93

1	2
ended	bends
vended	ends

D 94

1	2	3	4	♥
cents	center	invention	as-cen-sion	non-sense
rents	renter	intention		in-cense

D 95

1	2
accepting	exception

DERIVATIVES

D 96

blessed	recessed	presses	lesson	co-a-lesce
dressed	depressed	messes		spec-i-men
1	2	3	4	♥

D 97

echelon
1

D 98

pester	Sylvester	testimony	festival	nestling
jester				
	in-vest-ment	nests	pest	ques-tion
1	2	3	4	5

D 99

betting	debtor	bets	petty	vet-er-in-ar-i-an
getting		lets		vet-er-an
1	2	3	4	♥

D 100

etches
fetches
1

D 101

deaths
breaths
1

D 102

Texas	per-plex-es	sexes	texts
	re-flex-es	vexes	
1	2	3	4

Ē

D 103

1	2	3	♥
ae-gis Phoe-nix en-cy-clo-pe-di-a (*also* en-cy-clo-pae-di-a) ar-chae-ol-o-gy Cae-sar	knee-pad free-dom	bron-chi-al people	a-moe-ba pae-an zuc-chi-ni tor-ti-lla

D 104

1	2	3	4
shil-le-lagh mos-qui-to	skis sei-zure	peas lei-sure	keys es-prit

D 105

1	2	3
reaching preaching	reaches preaches	bleachers

D 106

1	2	3
Pied-mont	feeding	weeding

D 107

1
leads reads

D 108

1	2
fa-ti-guing in-tri-guing	fa-ti-ga-ble

DERIVATIVES

D 109

1	2	3	4
be-lieve grieve re-lieve	thiev-ery	griev-ous	mis-chie-vous a-per-i-tif
leaves sheaves (*also* sheafs)	chiefs	thieves	griev-ing

D 110

1	2
meekness	seeks weeks

D 111

1
freaks speaks

D 112

1	2
te-qui-la	eels wheels

D 113

1
deals heals

D 114

1
fields shields

D 115

1
reams dreams

D 116	seems redeems 1			
D 117	beans means 1			
D 118	wie-ner 1	green-ery 2	scen-ery 3	queens screens 4
D 119	steeple 1			
D 120	heaps leaps 1			
D 121	creases 1	nieces 2	peace-able 3	
D 122	east-ward 1	priest-ly 2	beasts feasts 3	
D 123	eats meats 1	eating 2	neatly 3	
D 124	beets 1	completes 2	ath-le-tic 3	

D 127

leaving cleaving	griev-ance
1	2

D 128

easing pleasing	seizing	sneezing	tra-peze
1	2	3	4

R̃

D 132

spur-ring	in-curred	in-currence	in-terred	
stir-ring			a-verred	in-ference
	oc-curred	oc-currence	de-terred	con-ference
	con-curred	con-currence	con-ferred	ref-erence
	re-curred	re-currence	in-ferred	def-erence
	de-murred		de-ferred	pref-erence
en-tered			trans-ferred	
mus-tered				
	ogre		scler-o-sis	en-trance
ker-nel	eu-chre		cir-rho-sis	suf-fer-ance
col-o-nel	mas-sa-cre	scurry		
	thea-tre			
	(*or* thea-ter)			
	mar-tyr			
1	2	3	4	♥

D 133

curbing disturbing	verbs	curbs
1	2	3

D 134	birches 1	churches 2	perches 3	searches 4	
D 135	birds 1	herds 2	words 3	cup-board 4	
D 136	surfing 1				
D 137	merging 1	surging 2	scour-ging 3		
D 138	perking lurking irking 1	clerks lurks works 2			
D 139	cur-ling 1	twir-ling 2	pearls 3	twirls 4	furls ♥
D 140	firming 1	squirms 2	germs 3		
D 141	burns 1	earns 2	churning 3	yearning 4	journey ♥
D 142	burping slurping 1	chirps 2	twerps 3	blurbs 4	

DERIVATIVES

D 143	nursing	rehearsing
	1	2

D 144					
	ex-er-tion	skir-ting	dirty	hertz	a-ver-sion
	de-ser-tion			hurts	
	con-ver-sion				
	1	2	3	4	5

D 145	worthy	birthday
	1	2

D 147		ner-vous	pre-ser-vation	con-ser-va-to-ry
			ob-ser-vation	ob-ser-va-to-ry
	serving		re-ser-vation	
	curving			hors d'oeuvres
	1	2	3	4

Ĭ

D 148	fib-bing	sib-ling	nib-ble	bibs
	rib-bing			cribs
	1	2	3	4

D 149	bricks	pic-nic
	kicks	pic-nick-ing
	1	2

D 150	stric-tures	ad-dic-tion	convicts
		pre-dic-tion	
		re-stric-tion	
	1	2	3

D 151	vic-tuals 1	bidden hidden 2	kidding skidding 3	rigid frigid 4	salad 5
D 152	hem-or-rhage 1	bridging 2	pigeon 3		
D 153	tariff sheriff 1	cliffs sniffs 2			
D 154	drifts gifts 1				
D 155	bigger rigger 1	brig-a-dier 2	pigs swigs 3		
D 156	ful-fill (*or* ful-fil) will-ful (*or* wil-ful) 1	gills pills 2	film 4	kiln ♥	
D 157	filches 1				
D 158	builds 1	building 2			
D 159	bilks silks 1				

DERIVATIVES

D 160
stilts wilts
1

D 161			
limbo	hym-nal	dim-ming swim-ming	gym-na-si-um
1	2	3	4

D 162
limps scrimps
1

D 163				
o-cean	grinning winning	for-eign	cin-na-mon	com-mon
1	2	3	4	5

D 164	
mincing	con-science
1	2

D 165	
inches	lynches
1	2

D 166	
in-fringing im-pinging	in-fringe-ment
1	2

D 167	
hints prints	squinting sprinting
1	2

D 168

1	2	3	4	♥
equip equip-ped equip-ment	dipped flipped	lip-stick	tips	gyps

D 170

1	2	3	4
hisses kisses	listen (*silent t*) glyc-er-in	no-tice ser-vice	no-tice-able ser-vice-able

D 171

1	2	3
dishes wishes	fish (*or* fishes)	vi-cious de-li-cious

D 172

1	2	3	4
risky frisky	whiskey (*or* whisky)	discus	risks whisks

D 175

1	2	3	4
his-to-ry	mys-ti-cal	mys-tery	ir-re-sis-ti-ble

D 176

1	2	3	4
knitted admitted	kitten mitten	ad-mis-sible per-mis-sible	ben-e-fit-ed (*or* ben-e-fit-ted)

D 177

1	2	3	4
sand-wich	witch-craft hitch-hike	itches ditches pitcher	riches

D 178

Smith	: *singular*
Smiths	: *plural*
Smith's	: *singular possessive*
Smiths'	: *plural possessive*
1	

D 179

fixes sixes	6s
1	2

D 180

fizzing quizzing whizzing	scis-sors	frizzle sizzle	fizzes frizzes	quizzes whizzes	bus-i-ness busy
1	2	3	4	♥	6

ŋ

D 181

sings swings	ging-ham
1	2

D 182

stinks drinks ♥	Lincoln
1	2

D 183

tinc-ture
1

D 184	jinxes minxes 1	(*plural*--lynx *or* lynxes) 2

Ī

D 185	skied (*or* skyed) 1	cried dried 2	flies spies 3	di-a-mond 4	coy-o-te is-land 5

D 186	dyeing eyeing (*or* eying) 1	buying 2

D 187	sighs thighs 1

D 188				
mae-stro 1	kay-ak 2	dying lying 3	tying (*or* tieing) vying 4	gey-ser 5

D 189	bribing in-scribing 1	bribery 2

D 190	pricing enticing 1	police 2

DERIVATIVES

D 191	
	riding chiding
	1

D 192				
	ri-ot-ous	qui-e-tus	diets	riots
	1	2	3	4

D 193			
	rifle	Eiffel	lives (noun) knives
	1	2	3

D 194				
	Reich	biking hiking	likely	likable (*or* likeable)
	1	2	3	4

D 195	smiling filing	dialing	trials	miles	mileage (*also* milage)
	1	2	3	4	♥

D 196	children	wil-der-ness
	1	2

D 197	chiming	rhyming	crim-i-nal
	1	2	3

D 198	ninth miner diner	Veiner+ Steiner+ China	as-sign-ment a-lign-ment	dining lining
	1	2	3	4

D 199

kind-li-ness	binds finds
1	2

D 200

ripeness	wiping	typing
1	2	3

D 201

de-si-ra-ble
ad-mi-ra-ble
1

D 202

ex-cit-able ex-cite-ment	biting writing	po-lite-ness sprite-like	in-dict-ment
1	2	3	4

D 203

fights nights	light-ning righ-teous	light-en	spright-ly
1	2	3	4

D 205

diving driving	livery
1	2

D 206

paralyze	rising	prizing	seis-mo-graph
1	2	3	4

Ah or AW

D 207	bras-siere	bra-zier
	1	2

D 208	jobbing lobbing	mobs globs	goblin
	1	2	3

D 209	choc-o-late	knocking locking	docks
	1	2	3

D 210	plodding nodding	model	trodden	waddle	nods plods	solder
	1	2	3	4	♥	♥

D 211	dodging lodging
	1

D 212	ped-a-gogue syn-a-gogue	clogged logged	clogs logs
	1	2	3

D 213	mommy Tommy	bombing	bombs
	1	2	3

D 215

clomp pomp romp stomp	swamp
1	2

D 216

Connie	conning	donned	cons dons
1	2	3	4

D 217

drops hops	copy copies	choppy	topping swapping
1	2	3	4

D 218

joshes	ga-losh-es
1	2

D 219

al-lot-ted al-lot-ment	gotten forgotten	plotted potted	dots lots	squatted
1	2	3	4	♥

D 220

botches blotches
1

D 222

boxes (*pl.*, foxes *or* fox)	oxen	nox-ious	dachs-hund
1	2	3	

D 223				
	ga-ra-ged		bar-raging	
	1		2	

AW

D 224	law-yer Saw-yer	drawers	straws claws	aw-ful
	1	2	3	4

D 225	frauds lauds
	1

D 226	doffs scoffs	coughs
	1	2

D 227	often softening	lofts
	1	2

D 228	crawls shawls	bawling
	1	2

D 229	falls calls	hauling
	1	2

D 231	walks talks 1		gawks hawks 2		
D 232	hal-ter psal-ter 1	altar 2	falter 3	halts 4	faults ♥
D 233		waltzes 1			
D 234	ab-so-lu-tion e-vo-lu-tion re-so-lu-tion 1		sol-vent 2		in-volve-ment 3
D 235	lawns 1	awning 2			lin-ge-rie 3
D 236		haunches launches 1			
D 237	pi-quant 1		haunts jaunts 2		
D 238		bonds ponds 1			

D 239

longing	prongs
gonging	songs
1	2

D 241

bosses	saucing
crosses	
1	2

ō

D 245

	po-ta-toes		does (*or* doe, *pl.*)	sews
	to-ma-toes		hoes	
		hoeing	toes	altos
Peu-geot		toeing		pianos
Re-nault				so-pra-nos
pro-vost			bu-reau	
	pot-pour-ri		bureaucracy	
	(*silent t*)		yeo-man	
1	2	3	4	♥

D 246

buf-fa-lo (*or* buffaloes,		chauf-feur
(*also* buffalos)		
	ban-joes	
	(*or* ban-jos)	
beaux (*or* beaus)		noes (*or* nos)
bu-reaux (*also* bureaus)		goes
tab-leaux (*also* tableaus)		
1	2	3

D 247

	1	2	3
	glowed mowed	growing snowing	rows shows

D 248

probing
dis-robing
1

D 250

cor-ro-sive
1

D 251

col-lo-guing
pro-ro-guing
1

D 252

choking
stoking
1

D 253

oaks
1

yolks
2

D 254

1	2	3	4
controlled enrolled	rolls	bowls	bowled

D 256

1	2	3	4
holy	wholly (*also* wholely)	solely	consoling

DERIVATIVES

D 257			
	shoulder	folds holds	sol-dier
	1	2	3

D 258			
	jolting re-volting	volts colts	adults
	1	2	3

D 259					
homing ohms	foaming	combing	foams	poems
1	2	3	♥	♥

D 260
phoning honing
1

D 261	
hoping e-loping	soaps
1	2

D 262	
closest	grossest
1	2

D 263		
voting	noting	doting
1	2	3

D 265	
oats floats	gloating floating
1	2

D 266	growths 1	oaths 2		
D 268	nosy (*or* nosey) rosy 1	rosier 2	im-pos-ing 3	bureaus (*also* bureaux) 4
D 269	owns 1	groans 2		
D 270	coaxes hoaxes 1			

OU

D 271	schnauzer 1	bowing 2	vowing 3	plough-ing 4
D 272	owls growls 1	fouls 2		
D 273	towels vowels 1			

DERIVATIVES

D 274	mael-strom 1	Cal-i-for-nia 2	in-ta-glio (*intalyo*) 3
D 275		couches pouches 1	
D 276	clouds 1		crowds 2
D 277		pouncing trouncing 1	
D 278	rounds hounds 1		
D 280		clowns drowns 1	
D 281		housing espousing 1	
D 282		ousts jousts 1	

D 283

outing shouting	doubted
1	2

D 284

mouthing
1

D 285

powered	flouring
1	2

ŌR̃

D 287

forty	oaring	flooring	poured	warring	ab-hor-rence
fourteen	oars	doors	fours	wars	
1	2	3	4	♥	6

D 288

storing shoring	mort-gage
1	2

D 289

swords	boards	awards	hoarding	gourds
1	2	3	4	♥

D 290

	1
	corks forks

D 291

1	2	3	4
warms	stormy storms	de-form-i-ty	mis-in-form-ing

D 292

1	2	3	4
scorns	thorns	warns	mourns

D 293

1	2
di-vorc-ing	en-forc-ing

D 294

1	2
sporting	courting

OI

D 296

1	2	3
toyed	employee (*or* employe)	enjoyment

D 299

1	2
poi-gnant	coining joining

D 300

noisy	noisily
1	2

D 301

hoisting	re-joic-ing
1	2

a

D 302

shrub-bery	pub-lic chub-by	sub-ma-rine cup-board	sub-sti-tute
1	2	3	♥

D 303

buckle chuckle	lucky luckier	chucks	huckster	suc-cess-ion
1	2	3	4	♥

D 304

de-duc-tion pro-duc-tion ab-duc-tion con-struc-tion	in-de-struc-ti-ble	pro-duc-tive in-struc-tive ob-struc-tive con-struc-tive	ob-structs
1	2	3	4

D 305

muddy buddy	muddiest	bloody	study	huddle cuddle
1	2	3	4	5

D 306

blud-geon	judg-ment (*or* judge-ment)	prej-u-dice
1	2	3

DERIVATIVES

D 307

1	2	3	4
duffle ruffle shuffle	huffy fluffy	gruffly	rough-neck

D 308

1	2	3	4
buggy	slugs hugs	smuggle	snuggle

D 309

1
loving shoving

D 310

1	2
an-nulled	mul-lion

D 312

1
gulps

D 313

1	2	3	4
humming chumming	summer	scummier	tummy

D 314

1	2	3	4
crumble	plumber	num-skull (*or* numb-skull)	dumb-found (*or* dum-found)

D 315	gump-tion 1		jumping 2	stumps 3
D 316	bur-geon 1	sunning shunning 2	funniest ocean 3	nunnery 4
D 317	honey money 1	sonny 2	onion 3	
D 318	once 1		dunce 2	
D 319	bunches crunches 1		lun-cheon 2	
D 320		Rotunda 1		
D 321	bungle 1		lungs 2	
D 322		ex-pung-ing 1		

DERIVATIVES

D 323

bunks	dunks
1	2

D 324

grunts	punts	coun-try
1	2	3

D 325

upping	cupping	pupils
1	2	3

D 326

us	buses	trusses busses	hustle bustle	isthmus (*silent th*)
1	2	3	4	5

D 327

Russia	brushes	crushes
1	2	3

D 329

dusts
1

D 330

cutting	jutting	huts	scuttle	cutlery
1	2	3	4	♥

D 331

crutches	clutches
1	2

D 332

lux-ur-i-ous	lux-u-ry
1	2

D 333

buzzes	puzzle	cousin
1	2	3

U & OO

D 334

rouge	chews news	beau-ti-ful	ma-neu-ver rheu-ma-ti-sm pseu-do-nym	ren-dez-vous
1	2	3	4	♥

D 335

ar-gu-ing su-ing	queu-ing (*or* queue-ing) pleu-ri-sy	fuch-sia sil-hou-ette	nou-gats nui-sance	truly duly
1	2	3	4	♥

D 336

boos	zoos	ca-noe-ing	sham-poo-ing
1	2		4

D 337

cubing
lubing
1

D 338

mooches	smooches
1	2

D 339

foods
moods
1

DERIVATIVES

D 340

intruding
protruding
1

D 341

goofs
proofs
hooves (*or* hoofs)
roofs (*also* rooves)
1

D 343

re-buk-ing	u-ku-le-le (*also* u-ke-le-le)	spooking
1	2	3

D 344

ruling	duel-ing (*or* duelling)	fueling (*or* fuelling)
1	2	3

D 345

cooling fooling	schools pools	♥ fools
1	2	3

D 346

as-sum-ing	grooming	as-sump-tion
1	2	3

D 347

moons	balloons
1	2

D 349

trooping scooping
1

D 350

re-futing	re-cruit-ing
1	2

D 351

curing luring	con-nois-seur	pur-i-fy
1	2	3

D 352

tours	insures
1	2

D 353

loosen loosening	using
1	2

D 355

smoothes	soothes	booths+
1	2	3

D 356

ap-proves	moving proving	movable (*or* moveable)
1	2	3

D 357

us-able ex-cus-able	choosing snoozing	losing	Tuesday
1	2	3	4

Ŭ

D 358		goods hoods 1	liv-able (*also* live-able) lik-able (*or* like-able) 2	
D 359		books nooks 1		
D 360	pulley 1	bully 2	woolly (*also* wooly) 3	woolen (*or* woollen) 4
D 361		bushy cushy 1	cushioned 2	

SPELLING RULES

1. Single-syllable words ending in one consonant preceded by one vowel, double the last letter:

run + ing = ru**nn**ing
big + est = bi**gg**est
hot + er = ho**tt**er
bag + age = ba**gg**age

Accent on Last Syllable
re•fer' + ing = refe**rr**ing
re•gret' + able = regre**tt**able

Accent Not on Last Syllable
dif fer + ence = differ**e**nce
ben'•e•fit' + ed = benef**it**ed
(or benef**itt**ed)

Exceptions:
vo**w** + ing = vo**w**ing
ta**x** + ing = ta**x**ing

2. Words ending in one consonant preceded by two vowels do not double the last letter:

sail + or = sailor
wear + ing = wearing

3. Words ending in two consonants do not double the last letter:

debt + or = debtor
yard + age = yardage

4. Words ending in *-y* preceded by a vowel do not change their form:

keys
buys
obeying
paying

5. Words ending in *-y* preceded by a consonant usually change the *-y* to *-i*:

beauty + ful = beaut**i**ful
accompany + ment = accompan**i**ment
lady + es = lad**i**es
cry + es = cr**i**es

Exceptions:
shy + ness = shyness
lady + like = ladylike
cry + ing = crying

6. Words ending in silent *-e* usually drop the *-e* when adding a suffix beginning with a vowel:

divid**e** + ing = dividing	surviv**e** + al = survival
fortun**e** + ate = fortunate	abus**e** + ive = abusive

Exceptions (often to keep the soft **g** or **c** sound):

courage + ous = courageous
notice + able = noticeable
change + able = changeable
peace + able = peaceable
acre + age = acreage
dye + ing = dyeing
manage + able = manageable
shoe + ing = shoeing

7. Words ending with silent *-e* usually do <u>not</u> drop the *-e* when adding a suffix beginning with a consonant:

arrang**e** + ment = arrang**e**ment	forgiv**e** + ness = forgiv**e**ness
saf**e** + ty = saf**e**ty	sham**e** + less = sham**e**less

Exceptions:
acknowledg**e** + ment = acknowledgment (also acknowledgement)
argue + ment = **argu**ment
true + ly = **tru**ly
awe + ful = awful

8. Use *-i* before *-e* except (1) when immediately following *-c*, and (2) when the two letters sound like long *-a*:

After c	Long a	i Before e	Exceptions		
conceit	vein	shield	weird	foreign	ancient
deceive	weight	believe	either	sovereign	forfeit
ceiling	veil	grieve	neither	sleight	surfeit
perceive	neighbor	chief	leisure	height	seize
(1)	(2)				

9. Regular <u>verbs</u> add either *-s* or *-es* to make the first person singular form; <u>nouns</u> ending in *-s, -z, -x, -ch* or *-sh* regularly add *-es* to form their plurals:

cuts	torch**es**	box**es**	dash**es**
cows	kiss**es**	buzz**es**	gass**es**

10. Nouns ending in *-o* preceded by a vowel usually form the plural by adding *-s*:

studios	ratios	folios

11. Musical terms ending in *-o* form their plural, whether or not they are preceded by a vowel, by adding *-s*:

pianos	trios	altos	sopranos

12. Nouns ending in *-o* preceded by a consonant usually add *-es* to form the plural:

tomato	tomatoes	echo	echoes
potato	potatoes	motto	mottoes

Note: Some words have two forms (commoner form is listed first):

mementos or mementoes
cargos or cargoes
zeros or zeroes

13. Plurals of compound nouns form the plural by adding *-s*:

sister**s**-in-law	co-editor**s**	editor**s**-in-chief
passer**s**-by	teaspoonful**s**	cupful**s**
	(or teaspoon**s**ful)	(also cup**s**ful)

Note: Possessive form is always made at the word's end, regardless of how the plural is formed:

Singular Possessive	Plural Possessive
sister-in-law's	sisters-in-law's
editor-in-chief's	editors-in-chief's
mother-in-law's	mothers-in-law's

14. All plurals of proper nouns are formed by adding *-s* unless the noun ends in *-s*, in which case add *-es*:

Singular	Plural
Hall	Halls
Smith	Smiths
Jones	Joneses

Singular Possessive	Plural Possessive
Hall's	Halls'
Smith's	Smiths'
Jones's or Jones'	Joneses' or Jones'

15. Adjectives ending with *-ful* or *-al* become adverbs by doubling the *-l* and adding *-y*:

cheerful	cheerfully
wonderful	wonderfully
practical	practically
normal	normally

16. Words ending in *-ll* often drop one *-l* when adding a prefix:

fill / fulfil roll / enrol

PHONICS

CHARTS

Chart 1

THE VARIABLE Y

	Ē	Ī	Ĭ	R̃
by	ba**by**	**bye**	---	---
cy	fan**cy**	**cy**clone	**cym**bal	---
dy	can**dy**	**dye**	---	---
fy	jif**fy**	de**fy**	---	---
gy	---	**gy**ve	**gym**	---
hy	---	**Hy**att	**hymn**	---
ly	ear**ly**	**lye**	**lyn**ch	---
my	**Amy**	**my**	---	**myr**tle
ny	pen**ny**	**ny**lon	---	---
py	hap**py**	**phy**lum	---	---
ry	Ma**ry**	**rye**	---	---
sy	Bet**sy**	---	**syll**able	---
ty	emp**ty**	**ty**pe	---	---
thy	---	**thy**roid	---	---
vy	hea**vy**	**vy**ing	---	---
xy	---	**xy**lem	---	---
zy	cra**zy**	**zy**gote	---	---

Chart 2

BEGINNING CONSONANTAL DRILLS

b	d	l	m	p	qu
box	David	lion	man	pig	quickly
baby	dog	lamb	mother	python	quiet
batting	door	Larry	met	pal	quitter
bugle	dot	lip	mopped	pull	quill
book	digging	light	more	Peggie	quizzed
boy	dumb	let	mill	pennies	
biggest	don't	luck	most	Pattie	
bell	dull	lasting	mittens	Paul	
boat	dam	lap	medal	pajamas	
	dirty	late	Mexico	popcorn	
	dear	loop	maple		
	Dallas	lariat	Monica		

y	v	f, ph	t, pt	g^1, gh
yes	Victory	fox	Terry	go
yell	vote	fort	toys	ghost
yacht	vomit	fat	Teddy Bear	gas
yodel	Vicks	phone	turning	guess
yoke	voice	fix	tomorrow	gap
yummy	volume	phonics	told	get
yippee	veterinarian	Philip	table	guns
		furniture	Tunisia	gain
		first	tennis	Gale
		funny	tacks	gal
		physician	Ptolemy	give
		fell	teacher	
		father	ptomaine	

g^2, j	th^1	th^2	thr	tr
jelly	thorn	then	three	tree
Jerry	think	though	throw	trunk
Jackie		than	through	trip
George				trigonometry
Jill				trial
gem				trick
generous				
jet				
jersey				
gentlemen				

bl	br	cl
blow	brown	clown
blood	brains	closet
blunt	broken	clobber
black	broom	clock
blue	brace	click
blonde	brim	clutter
blink		club

pl	dr	fl	fr
play	drum	flop	frog
plow	drill	fly	frills
plight	drop	flow	France
plumb	drink	flap	front
plume	drain	flip	from

gl	gr	pr	shr	sl	sn
glove	grapes	practice	shredder	sled	snow
globe	grades	praying	shrimp	slow	snort
glad	grass	proof	shrill	sluice	sneeze
glorious	group	principal		slip	snap
glue	grow	printer		slap	snack

sp	spr	squ	st	str	sw
spill	springs	squirm	start	string	swing
spot	sprocket	squiggle	stop	strict	swipe
spuds	sprout	squid	stung	stripe	swap
spigot	sprint	squall	store	strip	swear
speaker			style	strap	swerve

sc[2]	sch[1]	sk	x[1]	x[2]	z
scarf	schedule	skunk	x-ray	xylophone	zebra
scar	school	skill	extra	xylem	Zeke
scab		skip	exchange	xerox	zero
Scot		skin			

w	wh[1]	wh[2]	r	wr	rh
wasp	whale	who	rat	wring	rhinoceros
water	whip	whom	rope	wrote	rhinestone
wallet	where	whopping	rip	written	rhombus
Wyoming	what		rung		
wonderful					

h^1	h^2	h^3 (often silent)
house	honest	Hubert
home	herbal	humor
honey		hue
Henry		
hopping		
heart		
hill		

n	gn	kn	pn
nut	gnat	knob	pneumonia
noise	gnome	knock	pneumatic drill
nurse	gnu	know	
nothing	gnaw	knot	
nails		knit	
navy		knuckles	

c^1	s^1	ps	sc^1
cellar	salt	psalma	scissors
circle	silence	psalter	
cereal	sale	pschent	
circus	salad	(p is often not pronounced)	
certainly	Sunday		
	set		
	so		
	soil		

c^2	k	ch^2	c^3	ch^1
cabbage	kitty	chemist	cello	chair
curtain	Ketchup	chimera		chums
comb	Kate	character		church
college	kiss			churn
cap	kite			chat

s^2	ch^3	sch^2	sh
sugar	chef	schilling	shark
sure	Chevrolet	Schubert	ship
			shop
			show
			shudders
			shoes

chr	cr
Christian	crib
	crab
	crock pot
	crumb

Chart 3
Initial Consonants*

B	Bull..........................
C^1	Celery(1)
C^2	Camel(2) ....
C^3	Cello (6) ....
D	Dog ....
F	Fox(3)
G^1	Goat(4) ....
G^2	Giraffe(5) ....
H^1	Horse ....
H^2	Herbal Tea ....
J	Jaguar(5)....................
K	Kangaroo(2)
L	lynx

Where are all the bunnies?

I'm so glad I'm not a sawhorse!

* Use with Chart 4.

Note: For Charts 3 & 4, similar initial sounds *identified by matching numbers within parentheses* sound the same.

Chart 3 (continued)

M	**M**onkey ....
N	**N**ut(7) .....
P	**P**enguin ....
Q	**Q**ueen..............
R	**R**at(8) ..
S[1]	**S**eal(1) ....
S[2]	**S**ugar(9)
T	**T**urkey(10) ...
V	**V**iolin ....
W	**W**asp(11) ..
X[1]	**X**-ray ....
X[2]	**X**ylophone(12) ...
Y	**Y**o-Yo ...
Z	**Z**ebra(12) ....

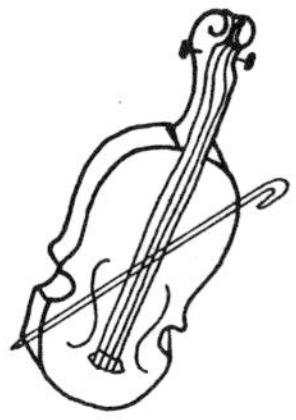

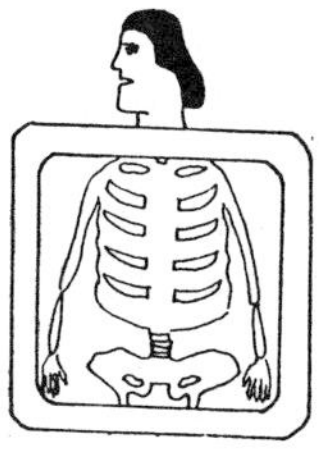

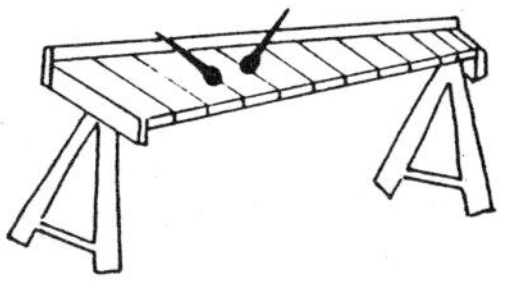

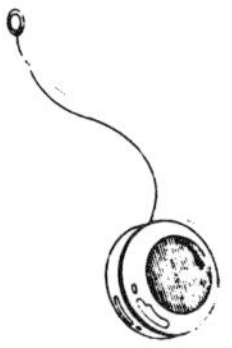

* Use with Chart 4.

Chart 4

Beginning Consonant Combinations *

BL	Blood Hound 
Br	Brood  ....
Cl	Clown............. 
Ch[1]	Church(6) 
Ch[2]	Chameleon(2) 
Ch[3]	Chef(9)  ....
Chr	Christ(13)  ..
Cr	Crow(13)  .
Dr	Drum 
Fl	Flag  ....
Fr	Frog  ......
Gh	Ghost(4) 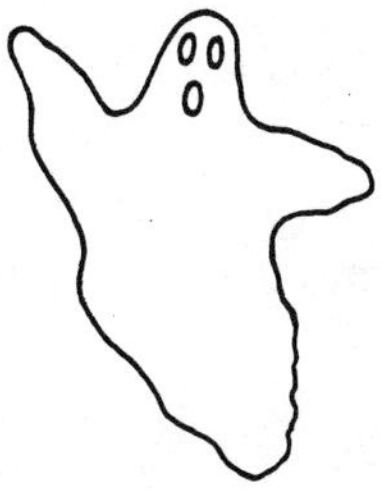 ....
Gl	Glove  ......
Gn	Gnats(7)  ....
Gr	Grapes  ....
Kn	Knight(7)  ...

*Use with Chart 3.

Chart 4 (continued)

Ph **Ph**one(3) ....

Pl **Pl**ane ......

Pn **Pn**eumonia(7) ....

Pr **Pr**ay ....

Ps **Ps**alm(1)

Pt **Pt**erodactyl(10) ..

Rh **Rh**inoceros(8) ....

Sc[1] **Sc**issors(1)

Sc[2] **Sc**arf (14) ...

Sch[1] **Sch**ool(14) ....

Sch[2] **Sch**illing(9)

Sh **Sh**ark(9)

Shr **Shr**imp ....

Sk **Sk**unk (14) .

Sl **Sl**edding ....

Sn **Sn**ail ....

* Use with Chart 3.

Chart 4 (continued)

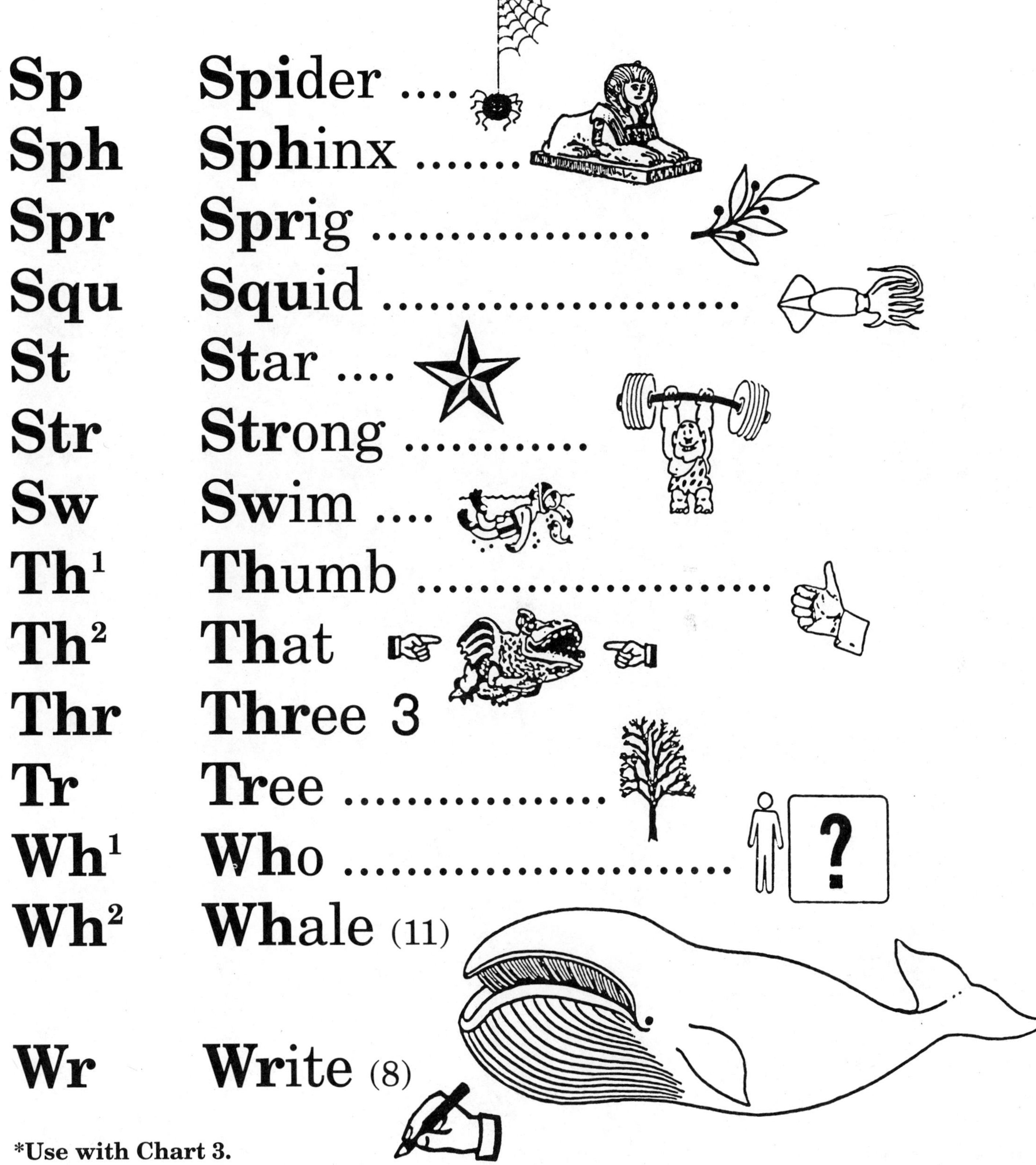

Sp Spider ....

Sph Sphinx ....

Spr Sprig ....

Squ Squid ....

St Star ....

Str Strong ....

Sw Swim ....

Th[1] Thumb ....

Th[2] That

Thr Three 3

Tr Tree ....

Wh[1] Who ....

Wh[2] Whale (11)

Wr Write (8)

***Use with Chart 3.**

About The Author

Tom McGann grew up in Washington, D.C., his home till 1989 when he moved to Huntington, Long Island (NY). After serving in the Army in Viet Nam he returned to college and received a Bachelor's Degree in Business Administration from the University of Maryland at College Park. Between 1980 and 1985 he wrote *Play On Words*, the original title of this book.

A couple steps were necessary before he would receive the required teaching credentials to enter a classroom to test the book's efficacy. So he returned to the University of Maryland. There, honing his reading and writing skills, he received a second Bachelor's Degree--in English (an "academic subject"); then he enrolled in a teacher certification program at the College of Notre Dame in Baltimore. He is fortunate to have taught 1st through 12th grades (including special education, foreign, and adult students). In Fairfax County, Virginia and in Montgomery County, Maryland, he tested *Play On Words* extensively, particularly with 1st and 2nd graders. And on various levels in several schools within the New York City Public School System, he has tested it further.

While earning a Master's Degree in Liberal Studies in TESOL (Teaching English as a Second Language) from the State University of New York at Stony Brook, he modified the book somewhat: a few stories are reworded, many more illustrations added, and the entire book reformatted--making it more enjoyable and much easier for both students and teachers. Next, to make the book easy for the user to follow on his or her own, he has had the book put on audio tape enhanced with music and sound effects. By summer's end of 1993 he will have fulfilled the New York State requirements for teacher certification in reading.

Ebullient from the success of *The Red Well-Read Reader*, Tom plans to teach monkeys to read next. He says, "The task shouldn't be so hard as one might think: the pupils are brighter than average, they are docile, and they show a keen interest to learn!"